T0004070

About the Authors

ABOUT HAPPY EARTH

In 2014, Happy Earth was born from an unmet need. The cofounders, Victoria Gennaro and David Winters, recognized that some of the brightest minds they encountered did not know about climate change. They decided that they wanted to educate others about environmentalism, nature, and the climate while using the resources that people actually connected to.

They launched an apparel line with nature designs and conservation mottos. Happy Earth is a social enterprise dedicated to being Earth first: with every decision they make, sustainability is the primary purpose. They built every aspect of their company around protecting the planet, from the details of how they make their products to their overall impact.

With every product purchased, they give back to create positive change. Combating climate change, planting trees, or cleaning up trash—the customer gets to choose the campaign they want their purchase to support. From make to mission, people and the planet come first. Connect with Happy Earth on Instagram @happyearth or www.happyearthapparel.com.

ABOUT THE AUTHOR

Kiki Ely is an author and wellness advocate. She has dedicated her life to empowering others to prioritize their physical, mental, emotional, and spiritual wellness so that they can find peace and purpose. She believes that a nonnegotiable component of this is an active relationship with nature. To share this knowledge, she speaks at retreats, conventions, and workshops, on podcasts, and online. She has penned numerous books on the subject, including *The Complete Guide to Self-Care: Best Practices for a Healthier and Happier You; Living Lunarly: Moon-Based Self-Care for Your Mind, Body, and Soul; The Complete Guide to Sleep Care: Best Practices for Restful Self-Care*; and *Find Your Peace: A Workbook for a More Mindful Life.* When she is not writing or teaching, she spends her time gardening, cooking, designing, and practicing wellness. If you would like to connect with her, you can find her on Instagram @blonderambitions.

adventurous SOUL

EMPOWERING WORDS OF WISDOM & STORIES FROM WOMEN WHO GET OUTSIDE

HAPPY EARTH *with* KIKI ELY

Brimming with creative inspiration, how-to projects, and useful information to enrich your everyday life, quarto.com is a favorite destination for those pursuing their interests and passions.

First published in 2022 by Rock Point,
an imprint of The Quarto Group,
142 West 36th Street, 4th Floor,
New York, NY 10018, USA
T (212) 779-4972 F (212) 779-6058
www.Quarto.com

10 9 8 7 6 5 4 3 2 1

ISBN: 978-1-63106-842-3

Library of Congress Control Number: 2022932416

Publisher: Rage Kindelsperger
Creative Director: Laura Drew
Senior Managing Editor: Cara Donaldson
Editor: Keyla Pizarro-Hernández
Cover and Interior Design: Tara Long

Printed in China

Contents

Introduction...4

CHAPTER 1:
Walk Your Own Path...6

CHAPTER 2:
Balance Brings Beauty...16

CHAPTER 3:
Change Is the Only Constant...26

CHAPTER 4:
Results without the Rush...36

CHAPTER 5:
Brave the Great Unknown...46

CHAPTER 6:
In Nature We Trust...56

CHAPTER 7:
Breathe the Wild Air...66

CHAPTER 8:
Live and Let Live...76

CHAPTER 9:
Sleep Under the Stars...86

CHAPTER 10:
Craving Wilderness...96

CHAPTER 11:
No Bigger Than a Grain of Sand...106

CHAPTER 12:
Keep Planting Seeds...116

CHAPTER 13:
Wander...126

CHAPTER 14:
Get Inspired...136

CHAPTER 15:
Say Yes to Adventure...146

CHAPTER 16:
Make Waves...156

CHAPTER 17:
Find the Calm Within...166

CHAPTER 18:
Connect with the Trees...176

CHAPTER 19:
Bloom Like a Flower...186

CHAPTER 20:
Thank Mother Earth...196

Make a Positive Environmental Impact...206

List of Featured Contributors...208

Introduction

The book that you are holding in your hands can change your life. This is because it contains a little bit of magic—the kind of magic that can only be found in nature.

Before moving forward, take a moment to connect with Mother Earth. If you are reading this outside, breathe deeply and look around. Feel the peace and beauty around you settle into your bones. If you are reading this indoors, you can either step outside to show nature appreciation or close your eyes and imagine a sun-dappled forest, a quiet range of snow-covered mountains, or a field covered in flowers.

You may have found that acknowledging nature left you feeling better than you did only moments ago. Perhaps you are breathing more deeply, your muscles are more relaxed, or your mood has improved. This is because nature is indescribably powerful. As nature is the focus of this book, you may find that the words inside have a powerful effect on you, as well.

In this book, you will read stories that will make you laugh and others that will make you cry. You will read about the lives of people whose journeys will make you reevaluate your own. Their stories will encourage you to be braver, kinder, freer, and bolder than you have ever been before.

You will find environmental time lines that help you learn about all of the ways that nature needs us. You will learn about all of the ways that we need nature. The impact of your existence on the environment—both the good and the bad—will become clear. Your knowledge of the steps that you can take to improve your impact will broaden.

You will come across sidebars that welcome you into the lives of prominent environmentalists. You might recognize part of your story in the story of another. The link that you have to Mother Earth will become apparent. You will learn about the interconnectedness of it all.

You will also find quotes that use the theme of nature to connect, ground, and inspire. You will be given the tools to experience true mindfulness in nature. Your past will become infused with peace and trust in your future will take root. Your relationship with the environment will deepen. You will learn how you can do your part to heal the Earth.

If you were not already a part of the Happy Earth community before owning this book, you are now. Happy Earth is a social enterprise dedicated to putting the planet first—and this book has the same mission. Happy Earth is committed to making conservation "accessible, fun, and fulfilling;" this book is an extension of that commitment.

Welcome, Adventurous Soul. It is so wonderful that you are here. Let our journey begin.

Walk your own path

1

A HAPPY LIFE
IS ONE WHICH IS
IN ACCORDANCE
WITH ITS
OWN NATURE.

—Seneca

LET'S START WITH A QUESTION: *Do you know who you are?*

In a sense, you do. You know your name. You know where you grew up. You know who your family is. You know where you live.

But do you know *who* you are?

This question is about the "you" who exists deep within. The "you" who existed from the moment of your very first breath. The "you" who is still wholly intact when you take the time to look inside.

If you feel disconnected from *who you truly are*, you are not alone. The noise in today's fast-paced world and the societal pressures that lurk around every twist and turn can be crippling to self-development.

The daily choices that you are making may not even be your own; they may be influenced by external factors that you are unaware of. You may be putting one foot in front of the other and walking the path that someone else has chosen for you.

Your path may have been shaped by love; this can manifest itself in the form of well-meaning parents or friends who want you by their side. Your path may have been directed by pain; this can appear in the form of heartless peers, a domineering boss, or a tumultuous relationship. Your path may have been directed without your awareness; this directional osmosis occurs in the form of lessons you learned in school, things you heard on television, or images you absorbed on social media.

If you are walking the path forged or chosen by another, you are out of touch with your truth. It can be difficult to identify your own path when there are path shapers, whether they be well-intentioned or ill-intentioned, surrounding you. This is why it is a healthy practice to carve out the time to be in solitary communion with yourself.

Nature is an ideal venue for this exploration.

While walking in nature, you are able to experience a peace that can be difficult to replicate in daily life. There is no outside voice telling you what to do or who to be; the only voice you can hear is your own. This space allows you to reflect, look within, and forge a deep connection with your authentic self. Walking your own path allows you to know who you truly are.

Nature is a seemingly magical portal to your inner truth. Once you are in connection with that truth, you will know your path. You will walk it with conviction.

National Parks Time Line

1872
The world's first national park is created

1916
The National Park Service is launched

1933
The National Park Service becomes responsible for protecting many historic monuments

1933–1942
Through the Civilian Conservation Corps, more people begin to work in and conserve national parks

2016
There are over 400 national parks and there is at least one in every state

Winona LaDuke (b. 1959)

NATIVE AMERICAN LAND RIGHTS ACTIVIST, SUSTAINABLE ENERGY & FOOD ACTIVIST

A Harvard graduate with a degree in rural economic development and a proud member of the Ojibwe tribe, Winona LaDuke is known for fighting for more than her people—she has fought for Native land. She is the founder of the White Earth Land Recovery Project, which seeks to buy back Indigenous land from non-Natives. This nonprofit also focuses on creating sustainable systems on the land and protects wild foods from becoming genetically engineered. Winona also helped create the Indigenous Women's Network, which consisted of more than four hundred Native female activists. She twice ran for vice president with Ralph Nader for the Green Party. She has been inducted into the National Women's Hall of Fame, was on the board for Greenpeace USA, and has authored multiple books about her environmental and cultural missions. She also fought the Dakota Access Pipeline to protect the water and the land of Indigenous people. She currently resides on the White Earth Reservation and grows heritage vegetables and hemp.

AS A NATIVE AMERICAN, WE SEE NATURE AS AN EQUAL AND WALK WITH HER AND NOT SEPARATELY.

—Samantha Yazzie,

ENVIRONMENTAL SCIENTIST AND SOIL LOVER

THE NAVAJO WAY OF LIFE RUNS THROUGH SAMANTHA YAZZIE'S VEINS. She grew up watching her grandparents exist in harmony with the Earth. While playing with her siblings and cousins, they would find dirt and put it on their tongues. Samantha loved soil.

When it was time for Samantha to leave for college, she wasn't initially sure of her path. Her moment of clarity came when she learned that she was going to be an aunt. She thought about climate change and worried that her niece wouldn't have a chance to see the snow.

She decided to study environmental science so she could care for Mother Earth for the generations to come.

Her childhood love of soil led her to a soil science class, where she learned about "carbon sequestration." When she realized that carbon could be captured by soil to heal the atmosphere and benefit the environment, she created an independent study to answer the question: Could carbon sequestration work for the Navajo?

She went back to the Navajo land, tested the soil, and realized it was possible to sequester carbon there. If the Navajo strategically rotated their animals it would improve vegetation, sequester carbon, and minimize the dust plaguing her people.

Now working for the Department of Agriculture, Samantha never forgets her people or her true path. She vows to bring her knowledge back to the Navajo to make her carbon sequestration solution a reality. This is her path home.

Balance brings beauty

2

JOY IN
LOOKING AND
COMPREHENDING
IS NATURE'S MOST
BEAUTIFUL GIFT.

—*Albert Einstein*

Achieving balance IS AN ADMIRABLE AND WORTHWHILE ASPIRATION.

However, you may find that your journey to inner peace is a frustrating endeavor. In large part, this is because it can be difficult to find an example of balance to emulate in modern society.

If you are to look to the media available to you for guidance on what balance looks like, you will likely end up confused and disheartened. The current trend is to promote a narrative of divisiveness, doom, and hopelessness. When you are convinced of the illusion that the world is a bad place, it's better for their bottom line.

The solution is to remove yourself from the unbalanced narrative construct of others and to see the world through your own eyes. This is the path to balance. It can be difficult to do when you are constantly bombarded with negative headlines and information. It can also be difficult to do when you are fielding opinions of family and friends, even if well-intended.

You must escape the noise and commune with your inner voice to discover your own narrative of balance. Your inner voice, or your place of internal wisdom, can only be accessed in stillness. One of the best places to access your inner knowing is while immersed in the stillness of nature.

Go outside and be slow and still. Engage your senses. Look at the plants and animals around you. Feel the sun on your skin. Listen to the breeze whistling through the trees. Smell the wet earth. Taste the fresh air. Then, look within. You will likely notice that you are more at peace than when you first arrived. Get used to the feeling. Let it settle in and become familiar. That's what balance feels like.

You can also learn the ancient art of balance from nature. Nature, when left to her own accord, achieves perfect balance. If you look carefully, you will notice that each element and creature plays a role, and each role is necessary to create a balanced ecosystem. When the ecosystem is balanced, it thrives. The same applies to your internal ecosystem: you must be balanced to fully thrive.

Once balanced, you can create and appreciate beauty. Flowers grow when they have the right balance of light, water, and food. When you are balanced, you have the ability to "stop and smell the roses"—or truly appreciate the flower. This is a necessity for a life well lived.

When you are balanced, you are able to see—and be—the beauty.

The Honeybee Life Cycle[2]

DAY 1
The queen lays an egg

DAY 4
The egg hatches and the worker bees feed the larva

DAY 10
The larva begins to spin a cocoon

DAY 22
The larva emerges as an adult bee and joins the colony

DAYS 22 THROUGH 43
The bee takes a role as a cleaner, nurse, builder, guard, or forager

Vandana Shiva (b. 1952)

INDIAN ENVIRONMENTALIST, ECOFEMINIST, AND FOOD SOVEREIGNTY ADVOCATE

Born in Dehradun, India, Vandana Shiva was raised by parents who were tied to nature. Her father was active in forest conservation and her mother was a farmer. She earned a bachelor of science, a master's degree in the philosophy of science, and a PhD in philosophy, specifically the philosophy of physics. She founded the Research Foundation for Science, Technology, and Ecology, which eventually led to a national movement focused on organic farming, fair farming practices, and the implementation and protection of native seed. This initiative, called Navdanya, has created more than forty seed banks in India and educates farmers on the importance of diversified crops. She has been called the "Gandhi of grain" because of her well-known anti-GMO activism. Vandana has also dedicated herself to the global ecofeminist movement. She believes that women have the responsibility to counteract ecological destruction. In 1993, she wrote her first book, *Ecofeminism*, outlining her ideas. At this point, she has written more than twenty books and been featured in numerous documentaries.

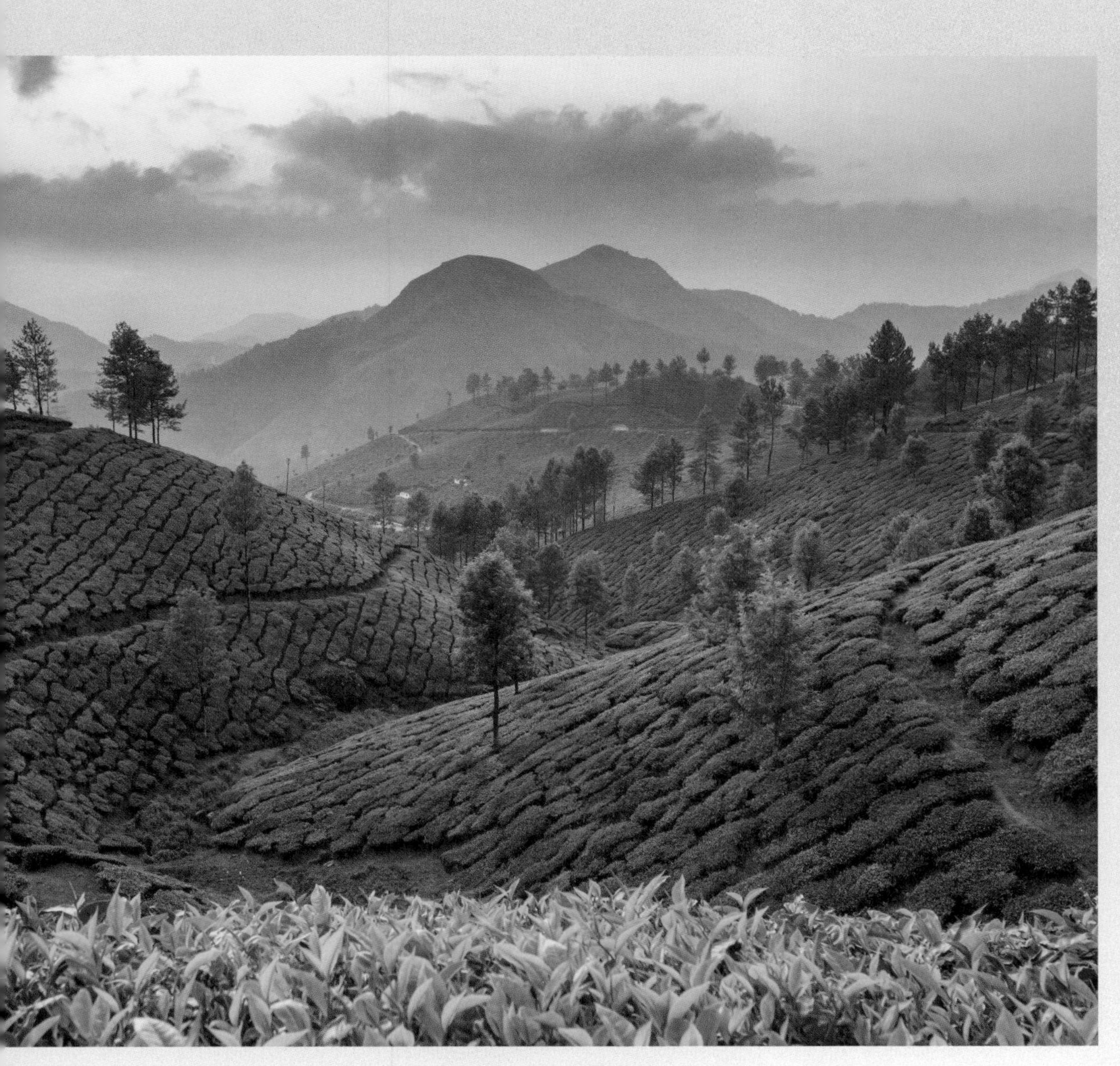

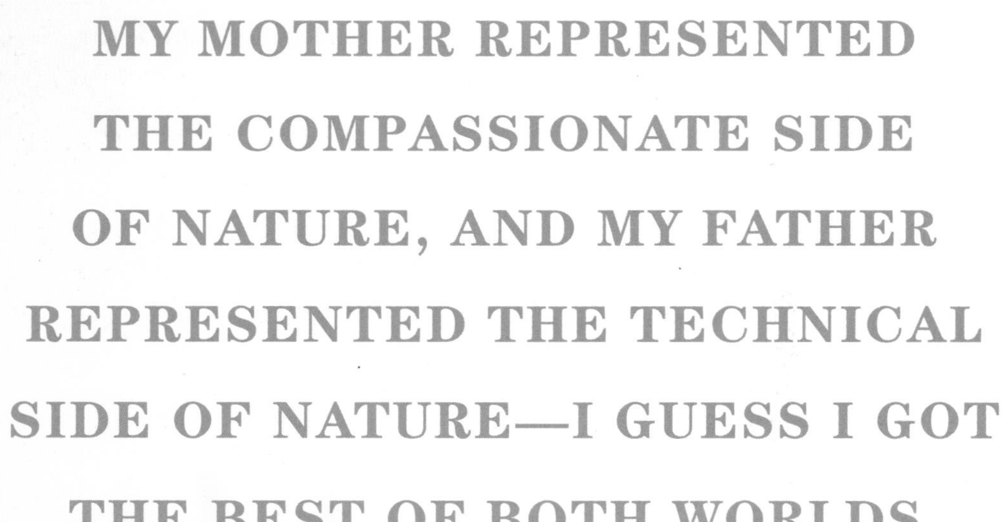

MY MOTHER REPRESENTED THE COMPASSIONATE SIDE OF NATURE, AND MY FATHER REPRESENTED THE TECHNICAL SIDE OF NATURE—I GUESS I GOT THE BEST OF BOTH WORLDS.

—*Suzan Chiang,*
BLOGGER AND MOTHER

SUZAN CHIANG'S MOTHER DEMONSTRATED COMPASSION FOR ALL LIVING CREATURES. Her mother's simple yet powerful lesson was: "Don't hurt nature." Suzan's mother taught her to respect and care for all of nature's inhabitants. Her father was from a family of farmers. He expertly filled their yard with fruit trees, flowers, and vegetables. Her father knew how to work with the earth, so everything he grew was organic.

When she was five years old, she began to take part in the family chores. Her earliest assigned task was to pull the weeds that grew in the garden. She would go outside on a hot summer day and try to check her weed-pulling chore off of her mental checklist.

Eventually, Suzan recognized that her little hands could remove a weed that was hindering a plant's growth. She was able to be gentle, as her mother had taught her, and precise, as her father had instructed. At that moment, Suzan found her balance. She stopped viewing her time in the garden as a chore and instead lost herself in the texture of the blades of grass, the breeze on her skin, and the sound of the birds.

Now grown and no longer a gardener, Suzan still finds peace in nature. When the demands of daily life begin to take their toll, she steps outside. Once outside, she is wrapped in the memories of all of the lessons that her mother and father taught her. Once outside, she is wrapped in memories of her childhood. Once outside, she finds her balance.

Change is the only constant

3

**NATURE IS
A MUTABLE CLOUD
WHICH IS
ALWAYS AND
NEVER THE SAME.**

—Ralph Waldo Emerson

TIME IS A *peculiar construct.*

There are moments in life when it seems to absolutely fly by. There are other instances where it seems to stand still. The relentless thing about time is, whether you notice it or not, it continues to march forward.

The clearest indication of time passing is a universal part of the human experience: aging. If you look at yourself in the mirror every single day, it might appear as though nothing has changed. However, if you look at yourself in the mirror only once a year, you will likely see some significant changes. If you only look at yourself once every ten years, you will see dramatic changes; you might not even recognize the person looking back at you.

In this way, time is synonymous with change. As time passes, you change. As time passes, the world changes.

This is precisely what is occurring in the environment around you. If you look around every single day, it might appear that not much is changing. However, if you looked at the same place once a year or once every ten years, you would notice a difference.

This change in nature can be caused by: 1) nature herself, 2) human beings working in harmony with nature, or 3) human beings acting in ways that are disconnected or harmful to nature.

To demonstrate this, imagine a forest burned through by a fire.

If this change was caused by nature herself, it can be beneficial. A forest fire can be caused by a lightning strike or spontaneous combustion. There are certain plants and wildlife that depend on fire to improve the health of the forest, clear out the underbrush, and create new habitats.

If this change was caused by human beings working in harmony with nature, it can also be beneficial. Controlled burns or prescribed burns have many benefits: they help protect the area from catastrophic wildfires, improve the health of the soil, and rid the forest of invasive plants.[1]

If this change was caused by human beings acting in a way that is disconnected or harmful to nature, the fire may have been started by a discarded cigarette, an improperly monitored campfire, or even as an act of arson. This kind of a fire can be wildly destructive. This is because these fires can occur too frequently to allow the forest to regenerate. This can kill flora and fauna, destroy wildlands, and disrupt animal habitats. Sadly, close to 85 percent of wildland fires are caused by humans.[2]

The good news is that if change is a constant, humans can choose to change things for the better. With more awareness, education, and thoughtful behavior, human beings can help nature continue to grow and change to reach her fullest potential. The same concept applies to you—as change is a constant in your existence, you can hone your education and behavior to continue to grow and change to reach *your* fullest potential.

Mount Shasta[3]

1820

Mount Shasta is known as a landmark on the Siskiyou Trail

1850

The first Euro-American settlements appear because of the California Gold Rush

1854

The first recorded journey to the peak of Mount Shasta occurs

1877

John Muir writes a popular article about the mountain

1887

The Central Pacific Railroad completes their line here, increasing tourism

EARLY 1900s

Pacific Highway is built, leading more people to the mountain

1976

Mount Shasta is declared a National Natural Landmark

Margaret Thomas Murie (1902–2003)

AMERICAN NATURALIST, CONSERVATIONIST, AND WRITER

The stepdaughter of an assistant U.S. attorney and the first woman to graduate from the University of Alaska, Margaret Murie is known as the "grandmother of the conservation movement." After graduating from college, she married Olaus Murie, who worked for the U.S. Bureau of Biological Survey. Her "honeymoon" was an eight-month expedition studying caribou in Alaska. As a couple, they would take trips and gather information about the wildlife in the area. They did this so that they could find areas that were worthy of federal protection. This led to the creation of the Arctic National Wildlife Range. They fought for the Wilderness Act to be signed into law; it was, only a few months after Olaus passed away. Margaret, known as Mardy to many, continued to fight to protect the environment. She was crucial to the passage of the Alaska National Interest Lands Conservation Act. She was also the recipient of the Audubon Medal in 1980 and the Presidential Medal of Freedom in 1998.

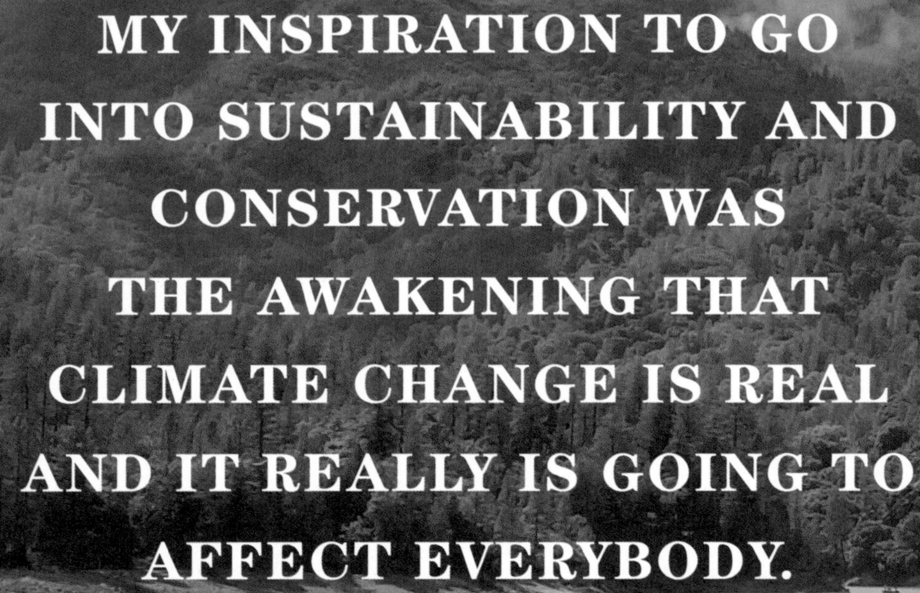

MY INSPIRATION TO GO
INTO SUSTAINABILITY AND
CONSERVATION WAS
THE AWAKENING THAT
CLIMATE CHANGE IS REAL
AND IT REALLY IS GOING TO
AFFECT EVERYBODY.

—Stormy Light,

SUSTAINABILITY ADVOCATE AND POET

EACH SUMMER, STORMY LIGHT'S FAMILY TOOK A ROAD TRIP from Arizona to California to Oregon to Washington. They stopped at national parks like Yosemite and Zion along the way.

Stormy found that her youthful insecurities were replaced with inspiration in nature. She would write countless poems about the beauty that surrounded her. She knew that she wanted these poems to reflect back on when she got older—just in case the world changed.

Her favorite part of the trip was the bridge to Lake Shasta. The water in the lake was clear and sparkling. The canopy of sun-drenched trees was lush and full. It took her breath away.

The summer that Stormy was fifteen, she approached the bridge to Lake Shasta. *Here it is*, she thought, *my favorite part*. Then, her heart shattered. The canopy of trees had been cut to stumps. Instead of a sparkling lake, she saw a dry and barren shell. The drastic change shocked her.

This moment changed the direction of Stormy's life. She decided to study sustainability and conservation. She is getting her degree in sustainability because she wants to be a part of the solution.

As she knew she would, Stormy enjoys revisiting the poems she wrote as a girl. Reading about the clear waters of Lake Shasta reminds her that, though change is constant, she can choose to enact a different kind of change—the kind of change that inspires action to heal, care for, renew, and preserve Mother Earth.

Results without the rush

4

NATURE DOES NOT HURRY, YET EVERYTHING IS ACCOMPLISHED.

—Lao Tzu

WE LIVE IN A WORLD OF *watches and alarm clocks.*

Our days are neatly arranged into inked events and obligations scribbled into boxes on a calendar. People operate within the confines of to-do lists and schedules. Efficiency is monitored by cold time lines of expectation ending in even colder deadlines.

The concept of time and its correlation to efficiency and expectation are purely human constructs. We have created the idea of years, weeks, days, hours, minutes, and seconds to chart and manage our existence. We actively track the time that has passed and attempt to plan for the time that is to come. This construct has built a mental cage of pressure and restriction with bars fortified by the illusion of time.

Nature thoroughly rejects our construct of time.

Nature does not have watches and alarm clocks—she knows all she needs are the light of the sun and the darkness of the night to regulate her rhythms.

Nature does not have a calendar—she knows that the seasons will come when they come and that she will have exactly what she needs when they do.

Nature does not have a to-do list or a schedule—she responds fluidly to keep herself in balance. To her, there is no past and there is no future, there is only the present moment.

Nature trusts herself to do exactly what she needs to do and to have exactly what she needs to have to be exactly who she needs to be at the present moment. Nature also trusts herself to become exactly what she is meant to become exactly when she is meant to become it.

Imagine if you adopted this attitude. You would be able to let go of things in the past because you would accept that what was, was supposed to be. This would eradicate feelings of shame, grief, regret, sorrow, blame, guilt, and depression. You would be able to let go of your attempt to control the future because you would accept that what will be is supposed to be. You would exist only in the present moment.

If you take away one big lesson from nature, make it this: your only responsibility is to respond to the moment in front of you *right now.*

If you greet your life moment by moment, you will transition to your natural state—that of a human *being*, not a human doing. If you allow yourself to meet each moment as it is and to trust that you have what you need to respond to it, you will become exactly who you are supposed to be exactly when you are supposed to become it. That's the thing about growth—it always happens at the perfect time.

Trust yourself the way that nature trusts herself. She knows that the results that are intended will appear at the exact right moment, so there is never any need to rush.

Environmental Action in the Early 1900s[4]

1900

A lawsuit involving pollution in the Mississippi River makes its way to the Supreme Court

1902

Ansel Adams, renowned nature photographer, is born

1904

Upton Sinclair's *The Jungle*, describing the pollution created by corporations, is published

1905

The first wildlife refuge is established by Congress

1906

The Food and Drug Act is made law by President Roosevelt

1907

Rachel Carson, revolutionary environmentalist and conservationist, is born

Ellen MacArthur

Ellen MacArthur (b. 1976)

YACHTSWOMAN AND CHARITY FOUNDER

Ellen MacArthur first received worldwide recognition for her achievement in yachting: she set the world record for the fastest solo trip around the globe. In 2010, she retired from sailing and launched the Ellen MacArthur Foundation. This charity's objective is to "accelerate the transition to a circular economy." A circular economy is designed in an intentional way to reuse materials and to reduce negative environmental impacts. The ultimate goal of a circular economy is to regenerate nature. The idea is to eliminate the concept of trash or waste and to instead circulate resources without generating any new waste. She has released two autobiographies, called *Taking on the World* and *Race Against Time*. Currently, there is a display about Ellen at the Wirksworth Heritage Centre in Derbyshire, England.

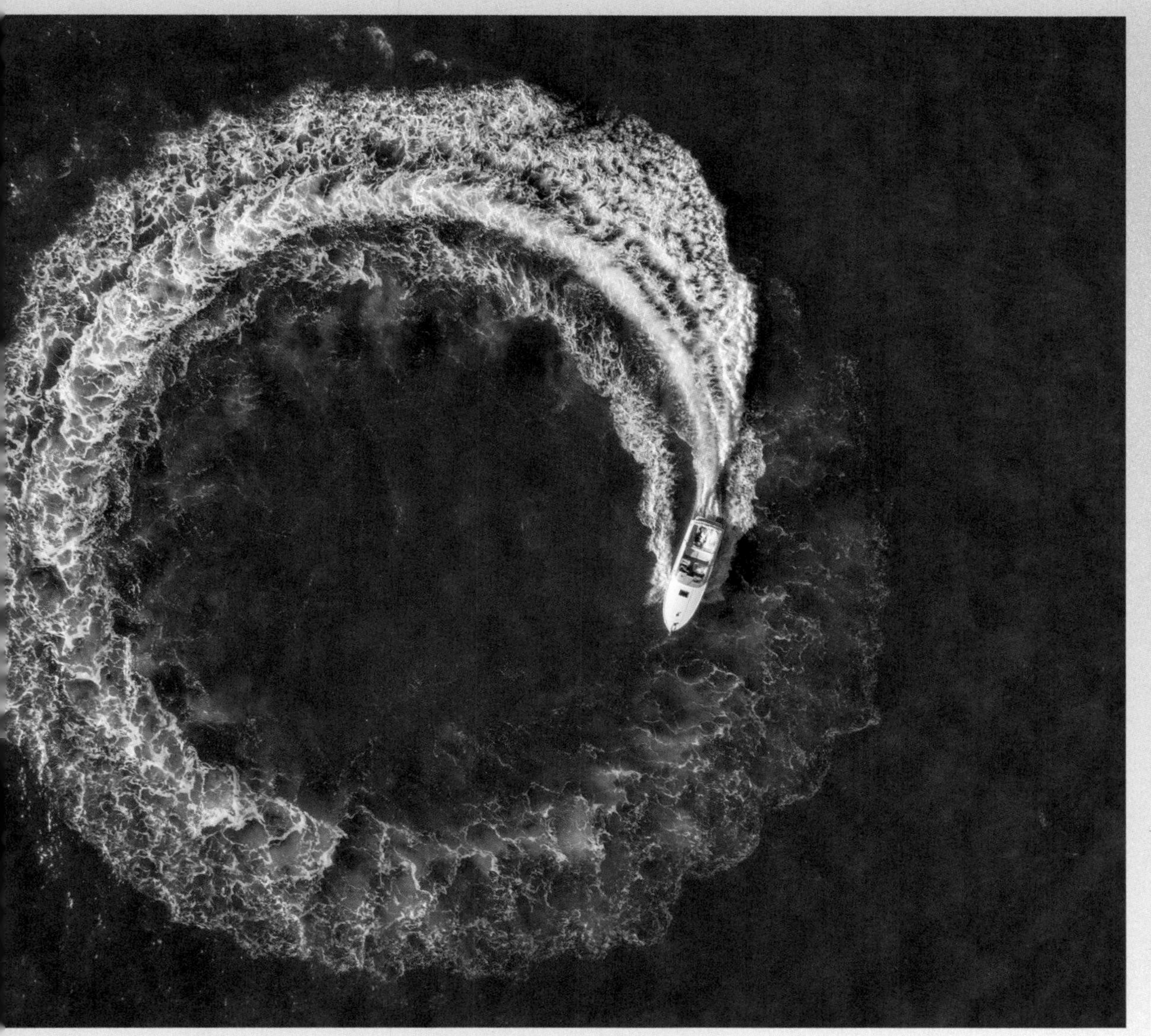

IT CAN BE EASY TO FORGET THAT NOT EVERYONE SEES NATURE IN THEIR EVERYDAY LIFE. WE HAVE TO LEAD PEOPLE TO HAVING A CONNECTION WITH MOTHER EARTH, OTHERWISE THEY WON'T KNOW WHAT THEY ARE PROTECTING. IT TAKES TIME.

—*Kaitlyn Lamb*,

NO-TILL GARDENER AND COMPOSTING QUEEN

A YEAR AGO, KAITLYN LAMB CLEARED A SMALL PATCH OF WEEDS AND PLANTED SOME CUTTINGS. Later, she received seeds from a teacher with an inspiring garden. Instead of waiting anxiously for the plants to grow, she created a compost system and built more gardening beds. She kept herself occupied with the present moment. With time, she watched her garden thrive; spinach, tomatoes, spring onions, lettuce, herbs, and flowers began to burst from the soil.

As Kaitlyn's garden grew, so did she. She chose to create a social media page to teach composting, sustainability, and the importance of organic non-GMO seeds to others. At first, she was unsure of what she was building, but she stayed wrapped up in what she was doing and continued to learn. As the months passed, she watched her community thrive; she connected with other gardeners, swapped seeds, and became confident in her gardening skills and her ability to teach others.

Kaitlyn wants people to understand their interconnectedness with nature. She believes that once people grasp their connection to nature, they will take care of her. She knows that when humans begin to grow their own food, they will understand that healthy soil creates healthier food, which results in healthier people. She trusts that she will someday see the gardens of countless people and their relationship with nature thrive.

She trusts this because she remembers what Mother Earth taught her: everything you need to focus on is happening in the present moment—things will thrive with enough time.

Brave the great unknown

5

THERE IS A PLEASURE IN THE PATHLESS WOODS, THERE IS A RAPTURE ON THE LONELY SHORE, THERE IS SOCIETY, WHERE NONE INTRUDES, BY THE DEEP SEA, AND MUSIC IN ITS ROAR: I LOVE NOT MAN THE LESS, BUT NATURE MORE.

—Lord Byron

WHEN WAS THE LAST TIME *you did something brave?*

Maybe the answer came to you right away because you're the type of person who would jump in front of a speeding train to save a dog stuck on the tracks.

Or maybe, like many people, you can't think of a recent example of your bravery because you cannot think of the last time you did something bold and brazen.

The key is understanding that bravery does not always show up in a dramatic and risky way. Bravery is the act of moving forward in spite of fear. This means that anytime you face, overcome, confront, or attempt something that causes you to experience fear, you are being brave.

If you have a fear of meeting new people and you quietly said "hi" to the cashier at the coffee shop this morning—you did something brave. If you have a fear of public speaking and you gave a holiday toast in front of your family—you did something brave. If you have a fear of crowded spaces and you took your niece to the zoo—you did something brave. If you have a fear of rejection and you asked someone to join you for lunch—you did something brave.

It does not matter whether the thing you attempted to do was successful or not. The mere attempt means that you confronted your fear, and that is the definition of being brave.

Now that we've reworked your definition of bravery, ask yourself again: when was the last time that you did something brave?

To live a truly expansive life, you can incorporate bravery into your day by stepping outside of your comfort zone. Your comfort zone is the space where everything familiar resides. The area outside of your comfort zone is where the unknown resides. This is also where fear lives. This is also where knowledge, experience, and joy exist.

Nature is a beautiful place to gently step outside of your comfort zone. Mother Earth has a way of softening many fears; she does not judge, she does not criticize, and she accepts you as you are. Nature is also a wonderful teacher when it comes to facing your fears. If you are afraid of heights, try to hike a little further each time you walk a trail that goes up the side of a mountain. If you are afraid of the water, start by dipping your toe into a creek before wading through a shallow pond. If you are afraid of the dark, try staying outside after sunset for a few minutes until you get comfortable enough to greet the night.

Take a cue from nature and start your journey into the great unknown.

Massive Volcanic Eruptions[5]

1815

Mt. Tambora in Indonesia can be heard from over 1,200 miles away and kills 71,000 people

1883

Krakatoa, at the Indo-Australian plate, erupts, causing a 140-foot tsunami that kills 34,000 people

1902

Santa Maria of Guatemala creates a 1-mile crater along the side of the volcano

1912

Novarupta, on the Alaskan Peninsula, results in 3,000 square miles being covered in a foot of ask

1991

Mount Pinatubo of the Philippines releases so much ash into the air that the global temperature drops by 1 degree Fahrenheit the following year

(1932–1985)

PRIMATOLOGIST AND CONSERVATIONIST

Dian Fossey is best known for her dedication to the mountain gorillas of Rwanda and for authoring the book, *Gorillas in the Mist*, about the time she spent with the apes. While studying gorillas in Africa, she learned that the apes were more comfortable around her when she imitated their behavior. This allowed her to develop close relationships with different gorillas to more completely observe their behavior in the wild. She founded the Karisoke Research Center to further the study of gorillas. In 1970, her work landed her on the cover of *National Geographic*. By 1980, she had received her PhD from Cambridge University and was viewed as the world's expert on the behavior of mountain gorillas. She started the Digit Fund to generate money to protect gorillas from being poached. Dian was found murdered in her research cabin in 1985. After her murder, the Digit Fund was renamed in her memory. Her amazing work has helped bring more global attention to the preservation of mountain gorillas.

AFTER SPENDING THE NIGHT
OUTSIDE ON TOP OF THE MOUNTAIN,
I FELT LIKE I COULD LOOK INTO
THINGS SO MUCH DIFFERENTLY.
IT HELPED ME OVERCOME MY FEAR.

—*Mugu Javad,*

PHOTOGRAPHER AND NEWLYWED

MUQU JAVAD GETS THINGS DONE. When she has a goal, she achieves it. When she faces an obstacle, she overcomes it. This rang true for everything except for love.

Romantic love had been a hurdle for Muqu. She had yet to find someone she trusted completely and refused to commit until she did.

One day, Derek—a man she was dating—suggested a sunset hike. As Derek was an experienced hiker and Muqu had never hiked in the evening, she was nervous, but she agreed.

Soon Muqu found herself surrounded by clouds. *This was a bad idea, we need to turn around*, Muqu thought. Then she thought, *But . . . what if I get to see an inversion?* Looking over the tops of the clouds was one of her lifelong dreams.

As they continued their climb, Muqu noticed that the fog and her mind had cleared. As the sun set, they settled on a cliffside. In awe, she stared down at the tops of the clouds beneath her.

As the sun disappeared, it became dark and cold. Muqu was surprised to find that she wasn't afraid; she felt safe with Derek. They stayed side by side on the cliffside all night, watching the Milky Way paint the sky.

As they descended the mountain in the morning, Muqu knew that the safety she felt with Derek meant that she trusted him completely. She was ready to commit. Now married, they look forward to all of the hikes to come.

In nature we trust

6

LOOK DEEP INTO NATURE, AND THEN YOU WILL UNDERSTAND EVERYTHING BETTER.

—Albert Einstein

THERE ARE CERTAIN ELEMENTS THAT MUST BE MET *for trust to exist.*

The first is consistency. When someone's behaviors, actions, and words are consistent, it makes moving toward a space of trust a true possibility. The second element necessary for trust to exist is that the person must not knowingly violate one of your boundaries. If someone knows that there is something you will not tolerate and they choose to do it anyway, this erodes trust. The third element of trust is safety. When around a person you trust, you should feel as if you are able to be yourself and share freely. If you find yourself feeling uncomfortable or concealing things, this is an indication that you do not truly trust them. The fourth element of trust is loyalty. If you tell someone something in confidence and they then tell someone else, trust will dissolve.

For a trustworthy relationship to exist, *both* individuals must be trustworthy. If you seek trust in your own life, you must first develop the skill of being trustworthy.

The following checklist of questions can help you determine whether someone is trustworthy. This same checklist can help you determine whether you are trustworthy—simply replace the words "Are they" with "Am I" and replace the words "Do they" with the words "Do I."

TRUST CHECKLIST

- **Are they consistent in the habits and behaviors I witness?**
- **Do they violate boundaries that I have set?**
- **Do they represent a safe space for me?**
- **Are they loyal to me?**

If you feel like you are having difficulty trusting yourself or others, you can spend time with nature to hone your own trustworthiness and to discern what it feels like to trust another. To do this, complete the following two sets of questions.

Go out into nature and find a space that is quiet, where you can be still. Breathe deeply and ask yourself:

- **Is nature a safe space for me?**
- **Is nature loyal to me?**

Then ask yourself:

- **Do I represent a safe space for nature?**
- **Am I loyal to nature?**

If your answers demonstrate that nature should not trust you, find ways to remedy your action or inaction toward nature. Perhaps you could be more consistent by spending more time in nature. Perhaps you could be more cognizant of how some of your lifestyle choices positively or negatively impact nature.

The more you hone your trustworthiness, the more you will be deserving and capable of being surrounded by those you trust.

EARLY 1900s

More than 100 million acres are plowed to plant crops

1905

Hugh Hammond Bennet, known as the "father of conservation," is hired as a soil surveyor for the USDA

1930s

The Dust Bowl sweeps across the region from Texas to Nebraska

1935

Bennet explains the Dust Bowl to Congress and this leads to the creation of the Soil Conservation Service, which is led by Bennet

1937

The USDA drafts the Standard State Soil Conservation District Law

TODAY

A conservation district exists in almost every county in the United States to work with landowners to protect, preserve, and restore the soil

Rosalie Barrow Edge (1877–1962)

NEW YORK SOCIALITE, SUFFRAGIST, ENVIRONMENTAL ADVOCATE, AND BIRDWATCHER

Rosalie Barrow Edge's first steps into activism occurred in 1915 with women's voting rights. She ultimately became the secretary treasurer of the New York State Woman Suffrage Party. In the 1920s, Rosalie fell in love with birdwatching. After learning about the killing of 70,000 Alaskan bald eagles, her interest in conservation emerged. In 1929, she founded the Emergency Conservation Committee (ECC). The concept behind the ECC was that all species of birds and animals should be protected, regardless of whether they are common, endangered, or financially valuable. In 1934, Rosalie bought a ridge in the Appalachian Mountains that had been used to shoot hawks and eagles for years and turned it into Hawk Mountain Sanctuary. Rosalie spent her life protecting birds, animals, and nature. She also helped create national parks and helped preserve 8,000 acres of trees in Yosemite National Park.

I ASK TREES FOR ADVICE, I TRY TO FEEL WHAT THE ROCKS ARE TELLING ME, I TALK TO ANIMALS AND ASK FOR THEIR WISDOM.

—Maggie Dewane,
WORLD TRAVELER AND WILDLIFE PODCASTER

WHEN MAGGIE DEWANE WAS LITTLE, NATURE WAS HER FRIEND. She loved to imagine that the woodland creatures in the forest behind her home were playing with her.

After she watched a children's show about extinction, nature revealed her purpose. The heartbreak she experienced led to her childhood declaration to "save the world."

During her teenage summers at an Audubon ecology camp, nature unearthed her passion: she wanted to teach others that humans, animals, and nature can exist in harmony.

When anxiety and depression joined her as a young adult, nature provided her with a refuge. She reclaimed her peace through walking pine needle–laden trails or breathing in salty ocean air.

After earning her master's degree in environmental science and policy, nature gave her a career. She worked for the White House Council on Environmental Quality, the Environmental Investigation Agency, an international nonprofit, and the Center for Progressive Reform.

Throughout her life, nature has been her companion. She and nature have gone to twenty-seven national parks on a conservation trip, backpacked across Southeast Asia to film wildlife conservation videos, and touched down on all seven continents. This led to a wildlife podcast, a film festival–featured short climate-change documentary, and a lifelong commitment to be a champion for positive environmental change.

Maggie is proof that placing your trust in nature and being the type of woman whom nature can trust in return can propel the most beautiful elements of life: inspiration, purpose, passion, refuge, a career, and a lifelong companion.

Breathe
the wild
air

7

JUST LIVING IS NOT ENOUGH . . . ONE MUST HAVE SUNSHINE, FREEDOM, AND A LITTLE FLOWER.

—Hans Christian Andersen

BREATHING IS GENERALLY AN *involuntary unconscious response.*

This means that it happens without you having to think about it. The unique thing about breathing is, unlike many other bodily functions, like your blood flow or hormone production, you can choose to turn breathing from an involuntary unconscious response into a voluntary conscious response.

Once you are conscious of your breathing, you are able to regulate the kind of air you are breathing and how you are choosing to take in this air.

Think about the *kind of air* that you are breathing. Right now, you might be reading this book indoors. If you are near an open window, then you might have access to some nice air. If you are in an apartment or office without operable windows, then you might be breathing recycled air. Right now, you might be reading this book outdoors. If you are at a cafe in the middle of a big city, you might be breathing visibly polluted air. If you are on your back porch in a rural town, you are likely breathing fresh air.

The kind of air you are breathing varies based on the toxins present and the level of oxygen available. When you breathe in recycled air or pollutants, your exposure to toxins increases and the availability of oxygen decreases. When you breathe in fresh outdoor air, your exposure to toxins is minimal and the availability of oxygen is optimal.

Think about *how* you are breathing. If you override your involuntary response, you can control how you are breathing to regulate the amount of oxygen you are receiving. When you take the time to consciously breathe deeply, fully fill your lungs, and completely exhale, you increase the amount of oxygen in your bloodstream.

This oxygen is important because it is what your body needs to function and heal. When you breathe, you inhale oxygen and nitrogen. This oxygen goes from your lungs to your bloodstream, where it travels to different cells to assist with breaking down nutrients to create energy. This energy allows the cells to perform at their best.

Additionally, when you breathe slowly and deeply, you activate the parasympathetic nervous system, which is essentially a relaxation response. The benefits of breathing this way can also extend your life by lowering both your blood pressure and your heart rate.[3]

The host of physical and mental benefits that accompany deeply breathing the wild air are astounding. If you want to assist your cells, improve your health, lengthen your life, and reduce your stress, all you have to do is walk outside and take a deep breath.

Carbon Capture Time Line[7]

EARLY 1970s

CO_2 is used in the United States for commercial enhanced oil recovery

1989

MIT creates a research program to develop technology for capturing and storing carbon emissions

2000

The MIT program results in the development of the Carbon Sequestration Initiative

APRIL 2000

The CO_2 Capture Project is formed through a partnership of eight of the world's largest energy corporations

2004

The CO_2 Capture Project enters its second phase

2009

The Global Carbon Capture and Storage Institute is created; their goal is to capture CO_2 and inject it deep into the Earth for storage

Marjory Stoneman Douglas (1890–1998)

JOURNALIST, AUTHOR, AND CONSERVATIONIST

In 1912, Marjory Stoneman Douglas graduated with a degree in English from Wellesley College. She briefly worked as a reporter at her father's newspaper before World War I. When the war arrived, Marjory worked for the American Red Cross in Europe. When the war was over, she returned to her father's newspaper and became an editor. This allowed her to develop her journalistic interests; she found herself concerned with the increasing commercial development that she witnessed in Florida. Marjory then pursued a career as an author. She wrote books focused on women's rights and environmental issues. In 1947, she published a best seller titled *The Everglades: River of Grass*. This book helped shift the minds of Americans to view the Everglades as worthy of environmental protection. This helped turn the Everglades into a national park, ensuring its preservation. In 1993, she received the Presidential Medal of Freedom. The conservation organization she founded, Friends of the Everglades, is still in operation today.

I WOULD DAYDREAM ABOUT RIPPING THE TUBES OUT OF MY BODY AND LEAVING MY HOSPITAL BED TO FEEL THE WARMTH OF THE SUNSHINE ON MY FACE AND FRESH AIR FILL MY LUNGS. WHEN I MADE THAT DREAM A REALITY, IT SAVED MY LIFE.

—*Kirsten Foss,*

FREEDOM LOVER AND DEEP BREATHER

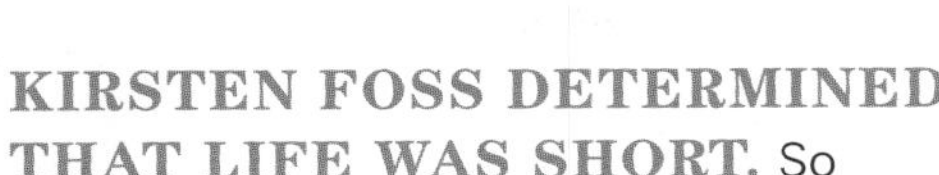

KIRSTEN FOSS DETERMINED THAT LIFE WAS SHORT. So she tried to do as much as she could—as quickly as she could. She didn't give herself time to breathe.

At sixteen, she left for college. By twenty-five, she was a lawyer, a model, and a businesswoman. By twenty-seven, she was traveling the world. At twenty-eight, she suddenly collapsed and was rushed to the hospital screaming in pain.

Fifty-seven days hooked to tubes and monitors, forty pounds lost, and more than one hundred puzzled doctors later, she still didn't have answers.

She talked to God, hoping he had an answer for her, imagining that he could hear her through the only window that connected her to the outside world. The hospital had sealed it shut—the fresh air couldn't get in.

Kirsten hated the sterile, bleached fluorescent air. She wanted to be with the air that had mingled with the sun on the other side of the glass.

She decided to leave.

As her mother wheeled her outside, the air hit her face. She took the deepest breath of her life. She could taste the sun.

God had an answer for her. He told her he could always be found where the air mingled with the sun. Kirsten knew this was where she, too, belonged. She had her cure.

She determined her life was long. She decided to breathe the wild air as deeply as she could—as slowly as she could. She vowed to always make the time to breathe.

Live and let live

8

WE DON'T INHERIT THE EARTH FROM OUR ANCESTORS, WE BORROW IT FROM OUR CHILDREN.

—*Native American proverb*

YOU HAVE LIKELY HEARD THE PHRASE "live and let live."

The idea is that you are entitled to live a life that is unencumbered by the opinions or input of others. It is a credo for personal liberty. However, it does not mean that you are able to do anything you want; the inclusion of "let live" at the end of the phrase means that your behavior *cannot infringe on another's ability to live a life unencumbered by the opinions or input of others.*

To understand this, you can think of two other popular phrases: "Do no harm" and "Treat others as you would like to be treated." Without this understanding, people may unwittingly live lives that encumber those of others.

Think of two people who both choose to start their day with a cup of coffee: The first person grabs their coffee at a drive-through window in a to-go cup. The second person ethically sources their coffee and makes it at home with a recycled filter; they drink it out of a reusable cup and use the coffee grounds and filter as compost.

Though both people get what they want, the impact—or "let live" element—of their choices is different. The first person may have purchased coffee that is grown using pesticides, their to-go cup might end up in the ocean, and their coffee grounds might get dumped in a landfill. These consequences can negatively encumber the lives of people, plants, animals, and the environment.

When you begin to apply the phrase "Live and let live" to anything that is alive, not just human beings, you can see the impact of your actions in a whole new way. You may not be able to see all of the far-reaching effects of your behavior, but taking a moment to think about it might lead you to make different choices.

Think about your daily habits and the small changes you can make to "let live." Perhaps you can shorten your morning shower by a minute or two to conserve water that is needed by other humans and animals. You might start composting your food scraps instead of throwing them in the trash, which would decrease methane gases in landfills that negatively impact those living near the landfill and the future quality of life of others. You might switch out your commercial meat sandwich at lunch for a salad or a sustainably sourced meat option to reduce animal cruelty so that animals have a better life. There are so many tiny choices you make while you "live" that can be improved upon so that you can give the gift of "let live" to other living things.

If this feels overwhelming to you, start small. Maybe you'll start with your morning coffee.

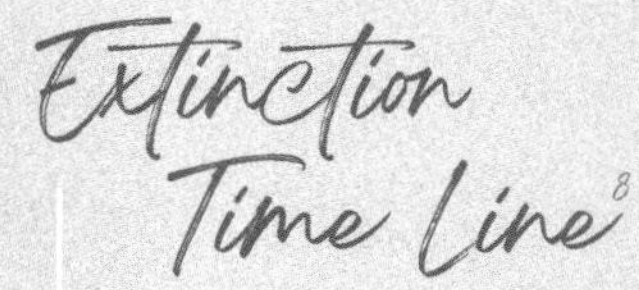

1690

The Dodo bird becomes extinct after pigs and cats are introduced into its environment

1768

Stellar's sea cow becomes extinct after being overhunted for its fur and oil

1900

The Rocky Mountain locust becomes extinct after its native habitat is converted to farmland

1936

The Tasmanian wolf becomes extinct after it is hunted, faces competition with domestic dogs, and loses part of its habitat

1989

The Golden toad becomes extinct due to global warming

Jane Goodall (b. 1934)

ENGLISH PRIMATOLOGIST, CONSERVATIONIST, AND ANTHROPOLOGIST

At only twenty-six years old, Jane Goodall traveled from England to Tanzania to study wild chimpanzees. She coexisted with the chimpanzees and lived among them to get an accurate scientific record of their behavior. She was able to identify that chimpanzees experience distinct emotions and that they form meaningful long-term bonds. In 1960, Jane made the groundbreaking discovery that chimpanzees are able to create and use tools. In 1977, she started the Jane Goodall Institute to support chimpanzee research and conservation. She has used her platform to educate people all around the world. She is currently a UN Messenger of Peace. She founded the Roots & Shoots program, a conservation education and action program that is active in more than a hundred countries.

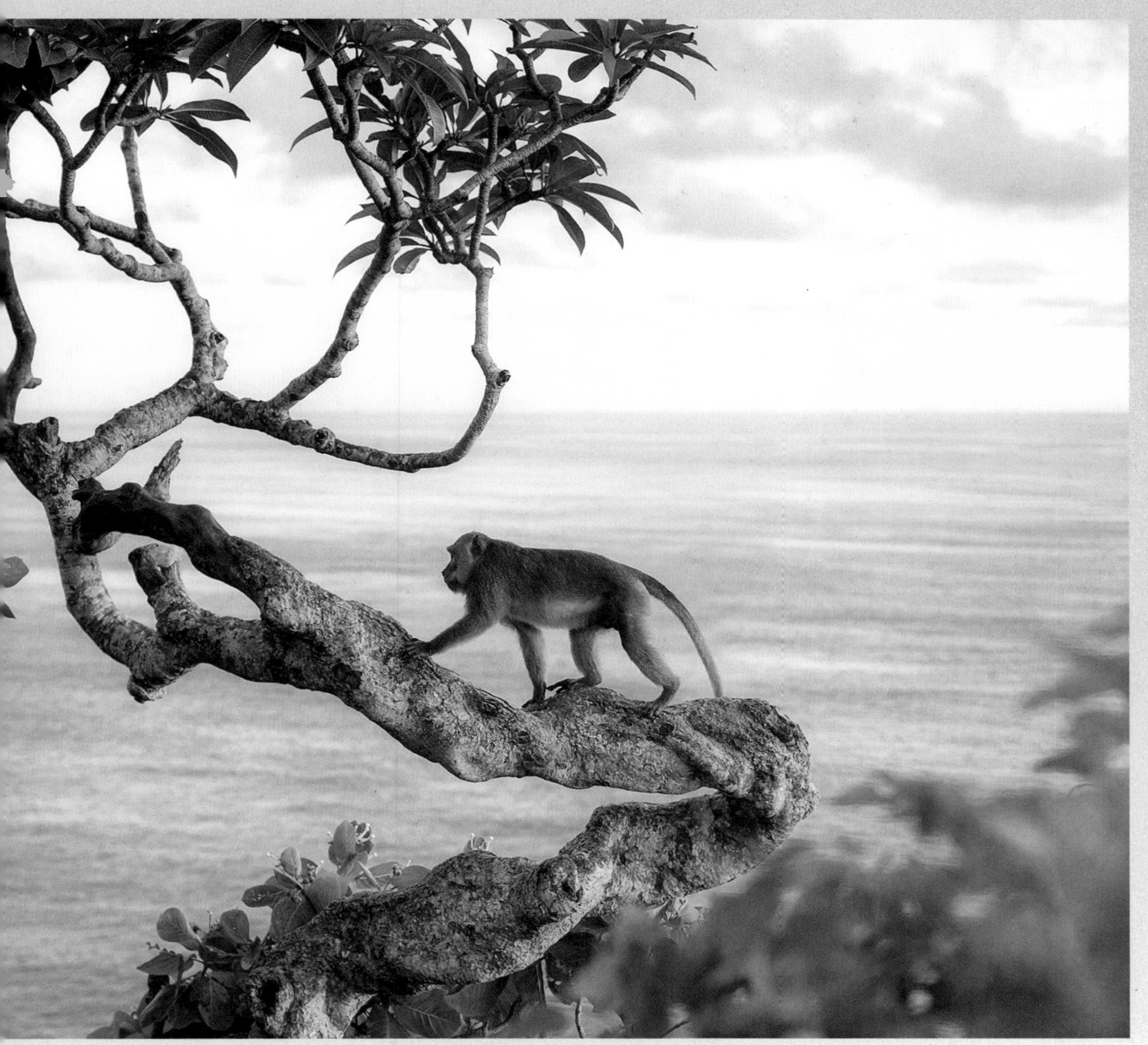

I HAVE STRIVED TO MINIMIZE MY IMPRINT ON THE EARTH BY CHANGES IN BEHAVIOR AND A FOCUS ON PERSONAL SUSTAINABILITY. THIS EXTENDS NOT ONLY TO LESSENING MY ENVIRONMENTAL STRAIN ON THE EARTH, BUT ALSO ENCOMPASSES ANIMAL WELFARE AND ELIMINATING ANIMAL CRUELTY.

—Danielle Lovett,
CHEMIST AND VEGAN

GROWING UP IN RURAL VERMONT, DANIELLE LOVETT WAS SURROUNDED BY NATURE. It was only after leaving her small town for the big city that she realized how she impacted nature—and how nature impacted her.

In the city, Danielle formed a close-knit group of friends. These friends educated her on the way her daily choices impacted the environment and other living beings.

Danielle made changes to reduce her personal impact on the lives of others. She bought a hybrid car, switched to reusable shopping bags, and was mindful of her water usage. She wanted to conserve resources for the environment and others. She also adopted a vegan lifestyle. She wanted to protect the lives of animals.

She was happy with the environmentally conscious life she had created in the city—and then the pandemic hit. Suddenly, Danielle felt trapped in a concrete jungle. To combat this feeling, she ran the river trail near her apartment every day. Soon, she understood the positive way that nature impacted her and realized that the city was not where she belonged.

Danielle moved to a place that bridged the gap between nature and the city: the suburbs. She lives her life in a way that is purposeful, constantly considering her impact on the world and its inhabitants—humans, plants, and animals. Living this way led her to a life that she loves and saved or protected the lives of and resources available to others.

Sleep under the stars

9

DWELL ON THE BEAUTY OF LIFE. WATCH THE STARS, AND SEE YOURSELF RUNNING WITH THEM.

—Marcus Aurelius

HAVE YOU EVER SLEPT OUTSIDE *under a blanket of stars?*

No, not in a tent.

No, not in a car.

No, not dozing for an hour or two before heading inside to the warmth of your bedroom.

Have you ever slept outside *all night long* with only the night sky as your ceiling and the morning sun as your alarm?

If you have never done this or if this experience is nothing more than a vague childhood memory of taking a pile of blankets into your backyard, then you absolutely should do it again. It is a beautiful, magical, and immersive experience. It is an experience that will put you back in touch with your animal nature.

It's funny how quickly—with the advent of modern society, technology, medicine, and architecture—human beings forgot who and what they are. We. Are. Animals.

To personalize this concept: *you* are an animal.

It only takes a few hours outside in the dark to be reminded of this. When you first enter the world of the night, you might feel disoriented. At first glance, there isn't much to see. Things appear to be uniformly black. As your eyes begin to adjust, you will notice shadowy outlines around you. As your eyes adjust further, you will be able to make out the clear outlines of the plants, trees, and objects that surround you. The stars will appear to shine more brightly. Your animal version of night vision has been activated.

While your eyes take their time adjusting to the night, you will have to rely on your hearing to alert you to your surroundings. Your ears will pick up sounds that you may fail to notice when you have the luxury of your daytime eyesight. You will hear the rustling of nocturnal animals in the trees sharply, the song of the crickets around you might sound like a loud hum, and the gentle rustling caused by the breeze catches your attention.

Certain plants emit their fragrance in the evening. The flowers that rely on bats and nocturnal insects for pollination release their strongest perfume in the dark of night. Your nose will begin to pick up scents from greater distances, as you rely on your sense of smell to gather information.

At some point, you may become comfortable in this environment and fall asleep. You will wake, like many other animals do, to the stunning light of the morning sun. You will feel in alignment with yourself and the day to come. This is the reward you receive for sleeping under the stars.

Landmark Environmental Documentaries[9]

1994

The Burning Season, about the Amazon rainforest, is released

2000

The Return of Navajo Boy, about the mining of uranium in the United States, is released

2004

The Future of Food, about the shift to GMO food, is released

2006

An Inconvenient Truth, about global warming, is released

2007

The 11th Hour, about environmental devastation and conservation, is released

2009

Food, Inc., about corporate farming and sustainable agriculture, is released

2014

Cowspiracy: The Sustainability Secret, about environmental corruption, is released

Sunita Narain

Sunita Narain (b. 1961)

INDIAN ENVIRONMENTALIST, WRITER, AND POLITICAL ACTIVIST

In the early 1980s, Sunita Narain coedited the State of India's Environment Report. This led to the important concept that protecting the environment is especially vital for the poor and that development interests might run counter to this principle. She cowrote *Towards Green Villages*, which demonstrated that democracies run at a local level are necessary for sustainable development. In 2005, she received the Padma Shri award from the Indian government. This award is very prestigious in India and is granted to individuals who make a significant contribution to the country. She has also been awarded the World Water Prize for her implementations of rainwater harvesting. Today, Sunita is the director general of the Centre for Science and Environment. She has 120 full-time staff who dedicate themselves to finding environmentally sustainable solutions to air pollution, water use, food and water safety, and climate change that they then advocate to become policy.

THE OKAVANGO DELTA IS SO ISOLATED THERE WAS ZERO LIGHT POLLUTION. THE NIGHT SKIES WERE UNBELIEVABLE. IT WAS A DIFFERENT KIND OF OUTDOOR EXPERIENCE FOR ME THAN ANYTHING I'D EVER DONE.

—Haley Coffin,

LOVER OF BIODIVERSITY AND MOTHER

HALEY COFFIN FOLLOWED HER LOVE OF BIODIVERSITY ACROSS THE WORLD to a study abroad, on a program in the wild and isolated Okavango Delta of Botswana.

The first days in the delta were very challenging for her. There were no bathrooms, no showers, and no electricity. She had limited human company, consisting of a couple of rangers and a scattering of other people. They were outnumbered by elephants, hyenas, and hippos. Instead of fear, Haley felt boredom. She didn't know how to pass the time.

Each evening, to help the minutes go by, she looked at the stars. The stars in the delta seemed to come from a completely different place than the stars back home.

Because the delta has no light pollution, Haley felt like she was staring into a vast universe dotted with infinite pinpricks of bright white light. She became captivated by the night sky and found that the time passed quickly while she was lost in her enchantment.

Stargazing helped her settle into the rhythm of the delta, like she was fusing with the pace of nature. At the end of her trip, she was saddened to leave the delta—she liked the way time passed there. She realized that the stars had synced her with the flow of life around her.

Haley left the delta carrying the knowledge of the stars. She knows that if she ever feels out of sync, all she has to do is slow down and look up.

Craving
wilderness

10

I PLUNGED EAGERLY AND PASSIONATELY INTO THE WILDERNESS, AS IF IN THE HOPE OF THUS PENETRATING INTO THE VERY HEART OF THIS NATURE, POWERFUL AND MATERNAL, THERE TO VEND WITH HER LIVING ELEMENTS.

—*Paul Gauguin*

Wake up. BRUSH YOUR TEETH. TAKE A SHOWER. GET READY FOR THE DAY.

Eat breakfast. Go to work. Work all morning. Grab a quick lunch. Work some more. Drive home. Change out of your work clothes. Eat dinner. Watch a show. Brush your teeth. Go to bed. Repeat.

If this routine sounds all too familiar, you're not alone. Maybe this isn't your exact routine, but you can see that your life is following a script that contains a similar repetitive pattern.

Without realizing it, life can start to feel like groundhog day. It is easy to fall into a mindless routine and to continue running in the rat race of life without taking a moment to look around.

It is when life starts to unhinge itself from meaning and purpose that the door opens for unwanted guests like depression, anxiety, and low self-esteem. These guests do not deserve a place in your life, but you have likely had an encounter with one or all of these unwelcome mental inhabitants.

You might unknowingly be allowing these emotional wrecking balls access to you by the way you live your life. You were not created for a life of boring, predictable routine; if this sounds like your current life situation, you are leaving the door wide open for emotional discontent.

Remember, you are a perfectly and intentionally made being who is here at this exact time and place for a reason. If you don't believe that, step outside.

Really—go outside, take a deep breath, and look around. Look at the sky and the trees and the flowers and the animals and all of the *life* that is happening around you. Isn't it beautiful? And vibrant? And colorful?

Yes, it is. And so are *you.*

If you are stuck on the endless wheel of purposeless routine, stop. Step off the wheel. Disrupt your routine with nature.

Carve out time, daily and intentionally, to spend in nature in any way you see fit. You can walk, sit, hike, bike, explore, meditate, or anything else that strikes your fancy. Your problems and pains that might seem so large when you are confined to the walls of your apartment, home, or office will likely seem significantly smaller when introduced to the infinite vastness of the great outdoors.

Your heart is craving the wilderness. That is where the prescription for your pain resides. Get outside and reconnect with who you came here to be.

Oil Spills[10]

1979

The Ixtoc 1 oil spill begins with a platform explosion that results in around 140 million gallons of oil pouring into the Bay of Campeche

1983

The Castillo de Bellver oil spill happens when an oil tanker catches fire and splits in half, dumping between 53 and 79 million gallons of oil

1991

The Persian Gulf War oil spill, the world's largest oil spill, results in somewhere between 380 and 520 million gallons of oil being poured into the Persian Gulf

2010

BP's Deepwater Horizon oil spill occurs after natural gas breaks a cement well cap, which causes a catastrophic explosion and results in 1,300 miles of coastline covered in oil

Isatou Ceesay (b. 1972)

GAMBIAN ACTIVIST, QUEEN OF RECYCLING, AND SOCIAL ENTREPRENEUR

Isatou Ceesay was born in a tiny village in Gambia. She received very little formal education, as she was forced to drop out of school as a young girl. At twenty-five, she founded the Recycling Centre of N'Jau to educate her village on the benefits of recycling plastic. Throughout the years, the organization has expanded to include teaching women business skills to turn plastic waste into recycled plastic bag purses from which they could earn an income. The organization expanded to include different communities around Gambia and is now known as the Njau Recycling and Income Generation Group. More than 11,000 people are part of this organization. Isatou has also worked for the U.S. Peace Corps, received the TIAW "Difference Maker" award, and been the subject of a book.

YOU CAN'T REALLY EXPLAIN WHAT IT IS OR WHY IT WORKS, BUT SPENDING TIME IN NATURE MAKES YOU FEEL ROOTED AND LIKE YOU AREN'T CARRYING THE UNIVERSE.

—Layna F.,
BURN ZONE ADVENTURER AND NATURE LOVER

GROWING UP IN COLORADO, LAYNA OFTEN WENT HIKING AND CAMPING WITH HER PARENTS. Her relationship with nature deepened as an adult. When making weekend plans, she found herself consciously prioritizing outdoor activities. She would hike new trails and visit burn areas covered by fresh growth. Seeing nature heal herself after such devastation was powerful.

Layna began to factor nature into her decisions. Her love of sunsets determined where she lived: western-facing with a view of the mountains. She added sustainable habits to her life one at a time.

Then Layna entered a phase in her life where she was feeling low and disconnected from herself, her family, and her friends. She couldn't find a way to pick herself up.

Layna decided to drive to a park. Upon arriving, she saw trash everywhere. She was heartbroken by the way others were hurting nature. She imagined someone else in her position arriving at the park hoping to find resolve and instead seeing trash. She couldn't stand the thought of them feeling the pain that she felt, so she picked all of it up.

With the trash removed, she sat down and watched the sunset. She closed her eyes and breathed in the fresh air. She suddenly felt rooted. She had received the hug from nature that she had needed.

Whenever Layna feels her soul start to crumble, she knows that all she needs is a walk outside or a glimpse of the sunset to come back to life. She knows that nature knows how to heal devastation.

No bigger than a grain of sand

11

IN ALL THINGS OF NATURE THERE IS SOMETHING MARVELOUS.

—*Aristotle*

NEGATIVE EMOTIONS HAVE A TRICKY WAY OF MAKING THEMSELVES FEEL *bigger than they are.*

Sadness, anger, stress, and fear can quickly transmute into their more destructive forms: depression, rage, anxiety, and terror. Because these highly destructive emotions have the ability to overwhelm our mind, they can feel all-encompassing. Once they feel all-encompassing, they can also feel really *big*. This is when it's important to understand the concept of perspective.

Think about your current perspective. If you only view the world through your own lens, then your experience appears to be the totality of what can be experienced. If, instead, you zoom out from your perspective to a wider lens, you see that what you are experiencing is only an infinitesimal fraction of what is actually occurring.

Imagine literally being able to zoom out, endlessly, from where you are right now. It would go something like this: You. Your home. Your street. Your neighborhood. Your town. Your county. Your state. Your country. Other countries. The world. The atmosphere. The solar system. The Milky Way galaxy. The Local Group of galaxies. The Local Supercluster of galaxies. The universe.

If you keep zooming out, you encounter the theory of the multiverse: the concept that the universe we inhabit is one of countless universes, much like we have learned that the galaxy that we inhabit is one of countless galaxies.

If it felt like your brain hurt when trying to comprehend the vastness of what is beyond you, it's because you were exercising your imagination. While "zooming out," you were attempting to conceptualize things you have never seen or experienced, like the idea of something infinite.

Imagine zooming out again, but this time you will start with things that are a bit easier to conceptualize. Start with a grain of sand and end with the world. It would look something like this: Grain of sand. Group of sand. The beach. The coastline. The ocean. All the oceans. The water-covered world.

This concept likely feels a little more familiar to you than the concept of an infinite universe, but it is virtually the same. To a grain of sand, the size of the water-covered world is just as impossible to understand as the vastness of the multiverse is to you. More importantly, to the water-covered world the grain of sand is microscopic, much like you are to the universe.

This is the magic of perspective: you can choose to shift from your view to a much wider lens of experience. Whenever negative emotions seem really big, zoom out.

Prehistoric Environmental Time Line

6000 BC
Communities in Israel collapse because of deforestation

2700 BC
In Mesopotamia, some of the first laws to protect forests are put in place

2500 BC
The king of Lagash moves water away from the kingdom of Umma, leading to the First Water War of Mesopotamia

1300 BC
Moses' proclaimed Hebrew law explains animal welfare and how to care for animals and slaughter them humanely

Hunter Lovins

L. Hunter Lovins (b. 1950)

AMERICAN ENVIRONMENTALIST, AUTHOR, AND SUSTAINABLE DEVELOPMENT PROPONENT

Hunter Lovins is the president and founder of Natural Capitalism Solutions (NCS). NCS is dedicated to assisting entities use regenerative practices that also lead to profit. Hunter believes that the model of capitalism can, when used correctly, result in profits and environmental gains. NCS has a vision of a future that is both profitable and sustainable. Hunter has written numerous books over the years; *Natural Capitalism*, a Shingo Prize winner, is her best known. She was also recognized by *Time* magazine as a Millennium Hero for the Planet and received the Trailblazer Award from the Women in Green Forum. She has been a consultant for a variety of industries, educational systems, and governments internationally. She is currently teaching social enterprise worldwide and is a founding professor of sustainable management at Bard MBA.

WHEN I LOOK AT THE GRAINS OF SAND ON A BEACH, I REMEMBER JUST HOW SMALL WE ALL ARE IN COMPARISON TO THE UNIVERSE.

—Kaitland Sweet,

PURE OF HEART AND MOTHER OF TWO

KAITLAND SWEET ROLLED HER NECK FROM SIDE TO SIDE. She did not know that "carrying the weight of the world on your shoulders" could feel literal until now. No one told her that grief weighed so much.

Her husband suggested they go on a train ride. She got their children ready and they boarded the train. The train began to move and she lost herself in sorrow-soaked thoughts of the mother and brother she had lost.

The sound of her son's voice brought her back: "Look! The beach!" The train doors opened and he looked up at her with a huge grin on his face. As if by magic, she suddenly saw things through his eyes. The beach was bigger than she had remembered. The ocean looked like it went on forever. And there was so much sand.

She spent the day as her children did: digging, splashing, and searching for seashells. As her son pressed a broken shell to his ear, she almost told him that they should keep looking to find one that was whole. Then he whispered like he was sharing a secret, "Listen, momma. You can hear the ocean." She smiled because he *had* discovered a secret: he could still hear the ocean in the broken shell because to him it wasn't broken, it was exactly as it should be.

She rolled her neck from side to side. The weight was gone. She hugged her son tightly. Suddenly, her sorrow seemed no bigger than a grain of sand.

Keep planting seeds.

12

A TREE BEGINS WITH A SEED.

—*Arabic wisdom*

LIFE IS MARKED BY *lessons learned.*

The peculiar thing about these lessons is that they do not always appear valuable when you receive them. The true value of a lesson does not appear until what you have learned is put into action.

Think about the following scenario:

A little girl loves her grandfather dearly. When she is very young, he repeatedly reads her his favorite poem by Rudyard Kipling. Each time he reaches his favorite line, he pauses for effect: "If you can meet with Triumph and Disaster / And treat those two imposters just the same . . ." She hears the line so many times that she memorizes it, even though she does not comprehend the adult concepts of triumph and disaster. Years pass. The little girl, now a young woman, loses her job. Shattered, she thinks, "My life is a disaster." The words that had been beyond her comprehension years earlier suddenly enter her mind and they *finally make sense*. She is able to put into practice the lesson her grandfather taught her: the "disaster" she is facing is an imposter and she has the power to change her perspective. Instead of viewing her life situation as a "disaster," she decides to shift her perspective and view the loss of her job as an opportunity to make an exciting life change.

A lesson learned is like a seed that is planted deep within you, the true value of which is only realized when the stem emerges from the soil.

Seeds travel by fire, wind, water, and animals. This means that plants can spring up in unexpected locations. If lessons spring up the same way, they may have been planted without your awareness. These are the kinds of lessons that you learn simply by living. Seeds can also be planted intentionally, like they are on a farm or in a garden. When these plants spring up, it is not a surprise; they were intentionally placed there. If lessons spring up the same way, they were planted with express intention. These are the kind of lessons that you learn in school or church. These are also the lessons you learn when you actively seek out information through books, documentaries, and lectures.

Nature also teaches us the way that seeds grow. The seed must move away from its parent plant to grow. This is because the seed needs its own resources to sprout and its own space to establish roots. You can think of yourself the same way. For your lessons to sprout and root, you must acquire your own space and resources; while you are dependent on others, you are unable to put your lessons into action because you are not making your own decisions.

If you incorporate this wisdom from nature, you will thrive. You will continue to collect and plant seeds throughout your existence. You will make sure that each seed has the space and resources it needs. Your field of life will be diverse, varied, abundant, and balanced.

GMO Time Line[12]

1935
Andrei Nikolaevitch Belozersky discovers DNA

1973
Man-made DNA, or recombinant DNA (rDNA), is created

1980
The first GMO patent is issued for a bacterium that can eat oil spills

1994
The USDA approves a delayed-ripening tomato for sale in grocery stores

1990
Over 100 million acres of GMO fields are operating around the world

Saalumarada Thimmakka (b. 1910)

INDIAN ENVIRONMENTALIST AND BANYAN TREE ACTIVIST

Married at the age of twelve and without a formal education, Saalumarada Thimmakka created a purpose-filled life that eventually earned her the National Citizen's Award of India. After getting married, she and her husband would graft saplings from the banyan trees in her village. They grafted and planted ten trees their first year. The next year it was fifteen. The following year it was twenty. They would carry water with them for miles to care for the saplings. Eventually, they planted 385 trees. She became known by the name of Saalumarada because it means "row of trees" in her language. Though her husband died in 1991, she continued to love and care for the trees. In 2019, the trees were threatened by road development. She urged her government to save the trees that she and her husband had planted seventy years earlier and they agreed. The BBC has listed her as "one of the most influential and inspirational women in the world."

IF PEOPLE IN HIGHER EDUCATION AND IN THE SCIENCES WHO WERE AFFORDED EVERY OPPORTUNITY TO STUDY CLIMATE CHANGE WERE STILL HESITANT TO BELIEVE IT, THERE WAS A MASSIVE EDUCATION AND OUTREACH ISSUE. HAPPY EARTH WAS SEEDED FROM THAT NEED.

—Victoria Gennaro, PhD,
BIOMEDICAL ENGINEER AND COFOUNDER OF HAPPY EARTH

VICTORIA GENNARO PLANTED SEEDS HER WHOLE LIFE.

When she was a child, her parents taught her about environmental conservation. She learned that her actions could help or hurt nature. The seed of accountability was planted.

When she was young, she went to nature camp. She learned that the flora and fauna that she loved needed insects for survival. The seed of interconnectedness was planted.

When she was a teenager, she explored the forest. She learned that a thunderstorm could bring the woods to life in a different way. The seed of adaptability was planted.

When she was in college, she studied biomedical engineering. She learned that she could use science to help others. The seed of community was planted.

When she was in graduate school, she did research in a laboratory. She learned that to find a solution she must fail repeatedly and learn from the results. The seed of perseverance was planted.

While spending hours in the lab, she would get distracted. She learned that engaging her body in nature brought her clarity. The seed of wellness was planted.

While working with scientists, she had conversations about the environment. She learned that not everyone believed in climate change. The seed of purpose was planted.

The seeds planted throughout her lifetime sprang to the surface. Her garden of accountability, interconnectedness, adaptability, community, perseverance, wellness, and purpose provided her with a path. This path led to the creation of Happy Earth, a business founded on these well-seeded values that focuses on social outreach, education, conservation, and sustainability.

Wander

13

IN EVERY WALK WITH NATURE ONE RECEIVES FAR MORE THAN HE SEEKS.

—John Muir

THE SAYING "NOT ALL WHO WANDER ARE LOST" IS A COMMON PHRASE, *but it might miss the mark.*

When it comes to wandering in nature, the saying may be better phrased as "most who wander are found."

Wandering technically means to walk without a set direction or purpose. This could also be rephrased as open-minded time spent in nature without expectation, yet open to all possibility and chance of exploration.

To wander is to walk much like a child does. There is a general beginning and ending point, but what happens in the middle is left up to chance and creativity.

Think of a family with a toddler attempting to leave their home. The parents likely have a set direction: exit the front door and get into the car. The toddler does not have this set direction. The front door opens, and the toddler enters the world. Instead of taking a straight path, the toddler may stop to look at a flower or jump in a puddle. They may find a bug in the dirt or be captivated by the dew on a spiderweb. They might decide to spin dizzily on the front lawn or see if they can jump high enough to touch the lowest branch on a tree. Eventually, both parents and toddler arrive at the car—but their experiences in getting to the car have been vastly different.

Though the experience and maturity of the parents may get them from point A to point B more quickly, did they demonstrate more wisdom than the toddler? The child's instinct is to wander. This allows them to discover and connect with their surroundings. This allows them to experience mindfulness, awe, and joy. It may take the child longer to get to the car, but they are full of wonder that the parents may have forgotten how to notice.

All they have to do to remember is to dedicate some time to wandering.

Because adults tend to have a lot more commitments and responsibilities than toddlers do, it can be beneficial to schedule time to wander. Add it to your to-do list.

Block out thirty minutes to go outside. No agenda. No plan. Just begin to walk and notice. If you are walking for too long in a straight line, you're doing it wrong. Noticing results in zigzagging, looking up and down, turning around, and circling things entirely to see them from every interesting and never-seen-before angle.

This exercise may seem confusing at first. As you lose yourself in the experience, the purpose of wandering will become clear. You will become engaged in the present moment. You will relax and breathe more deeply. You will be more aware of your surroundings and your interaction with the world.

The more you wander, the more you will find.

History of New York City Parks[13]

1733

Bowling Green Park becomes the first park in New York City

1836

Port Richmond Park, now known as Veterans Park, is the first park on Staten Island

1840

The Green-Wood Cemetery, with 478 acres and 20 miles of pedestrian trails, opens in Brooklyn

1847

Madison Square Park, Reservoir Square Park (now known as Bryant Park), and Washington Park (now known as Fort Green Park) are opened

1856

New York City acquires Central Park

1895

Brooklyn doubles its total park size

1968

The Parks, Recreation and Cultural Affairs administration is created

Kate Sessions (1857–1940)

AMERICAN LANDSCAPE ARCHITECT, HORTICULTURIST, AND BOTANIST

In 1881, Kate Sessions received a degree in natural science from University of California, Berkeley. She moved to San Diego to become a teacher, but soon left the profession. She then bought a flower nursery. This was her calling. Kate grew the nursery into a flower shop and then acquired other nurseries throughout the San Diego area. She entered into an agreement with San Diego to lease thirty acres of Balboa Park to use to grow flowers. The agreement committed Kate to planting a hundred trees a year in the park and three hundred trees a year in different locales in San Diego. In 1907, she cofounded the San Diego Floral Association. Kate passed away in 1940, but many of the trees currently adorning Balboa Park were planted by her. Today, she is known as the "Mother of Balboa Park."

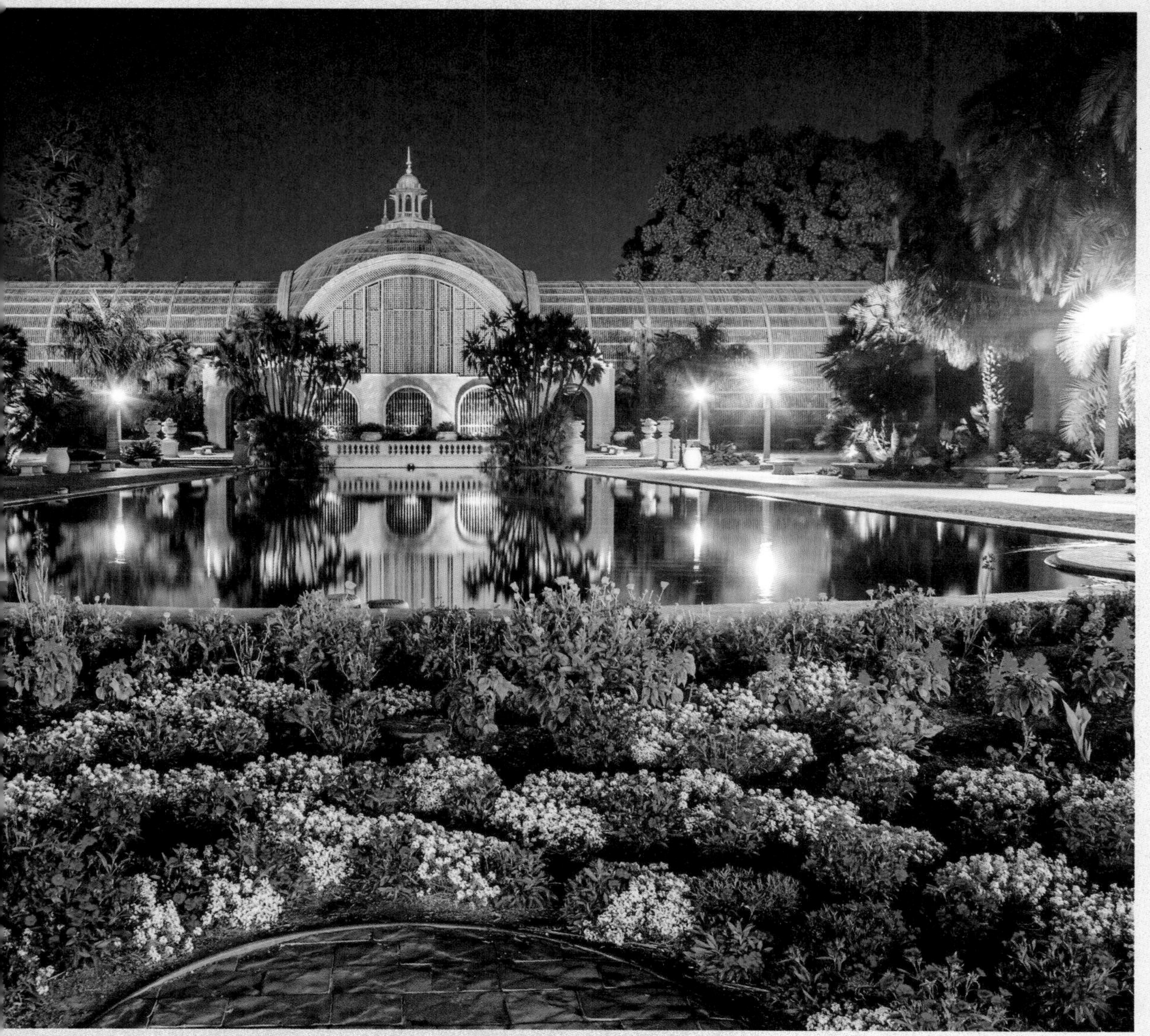

EVERY TIME I SEE SOMETHING NEW, I THINK THAT I NEED TO GO SOMEWHERE ELSE. WHEN YOU'RE IN NATURE, NOTHING IS THE SAME.

—Yvesanniah Lacoude,
EVENT COORDINATOR AND OFF-GRID WANDERER

YVESANNIAH LACOUDE LIVES A FAST-PACED LIFE IN MIAMI. A typical day in her life in the world of marketing involves fulfilling the roles of a community manager and an event coordinator. Her days are full of hustle and bustle: tours, keeping the common area organized, and managing seven different locations. Every other weekend she helps facilitate events for brands, companies, and CEOs. Her life is action packed, to say the least. That's why the choices that Yvesanniah makes in her free time might seem out of character. Whenever she has time off, she wanders into the middle of nowhere.

Yvesanniah loves to go off-grid so that she can experience space and solitude. She disappears with her thoughts and her journal. This is how she finds renewal. She feels like she "died and rose again" after time in nature. This time away is nonnegotiable because it is a wellness practice that keeps her balanced.

One of her recent getaways was a solo trip to a tiny home in North Carolina surrounded by small farms. She loved waking up with the sun and stepping outside into the crisp, cold air. She loved seeing the animals on her unhurried daily walks. She loved dipping her toes into the slow life before returning to the speed of Miami.

Yvesanniah dreams of all of the out-of-the-way and not-often-traveled places she will go during her free time. She is constantly dreaming of her next journey of renewal.

Get
inspired

14

IN NATURE THERE ARE FEW SHARP LINES.

—A. R. Ammons

ONE OF THE MANY BEAUTIFUL QUIRKS THAT SET HUMANS APART FROM OTHER SPECIES IS *the ability to create.*

Creating is different from making. Creating involves using inspiration and imagination to bring an idea into material existence.

Think of how truly incredible it is that some humans have the ability to see something in their mind's eye, imagine it in detail, and turn it into words, poetry, art, paintings, fashion, architecture, sculpture, and on and on.

Your imagination dwells within you, but what about your inspiration?

The word *inspiration* has a beautiful—and telling—history.[4] The meaning was derived from the Latin word *inspiratus*, which is the past participle of a word that means "to breathe into, inspire." In the fourteenth century, it was used to refer to the "divine influence" on someone. In the sixteenth century, it was used to refer to the process of inhaling air into the lungs. In the nineteenth century, it was used to refer to someone or something that is inspiring. These definitions help explain *where* inspiration dwells.

While your imagination lies within, your inspiration is found without and must be brought within. The fourteenth- and nineteenth-century uses of the word *inspiration* refer to beings—divine, human, or inhuman—separate from someone causing an effect upon them. The sixteenth-century use of the word means to breathe in. All of the meanings involve taking something outside oneself and allowing it access to the inside of oneself, where it has impact. This means that whenever you are feeling uninspired, you simply need to immerse yourself in an inspiring place and *breathe it in.*

Nature is full of inspiration just waiting to be acknowledged so that it can be integrated within you. Think of the awe-inspiring feeling that you have watching a sunset dip below the horizon. Think of the way that smelling fresh roses can make you feel. Think about the captivation you experience while observing a sky full of endless stars. Nature is full of limitless inspiration.

The imagination that you already have inside of you is simply waiting to be coupled with inspiration so that it can become creation. The more time you spend in nature and allow yourself to breathe her in, the closer you are to allowing your imagination to generate its full creative expression. Just think of everything inside of you waiting to enter the world.

Environmentalism in the 1990s[14]

1990

Nearly 76 percent of Americans refer to themselves as "environmentalists," according to a Gallup poll

1992

The international Earth Summit is held in Brazil

1994

The United Nations enters a climate change warning on their Climate Change Report

1996

WHO and the World Bank want leaded gasoline to be removed from society

1999

Seven out of ten scientists think that the current world environmental situation is leading to the largest mass extinction event ever

Biruté Mary Galdikas (b. 1946)

ANTHROPOLOGIST, PRIMATOLOGIST, AND CONSERVATIONIST

As a child, Biruté Galdikas's favorite book was *Curious George*. As a young adult, she learned about Jane Goodall's exploration of the chimpanzees and Dian Fossey's dedication to mountain gorillas. This propelled her to studying psychology and zoology at the University of California, Los Angeles. She earned her master's degree in anthropology. While completing her studies, she got to meet Louis Leakey, the paleoanthropologist who had been pivotal in finding funding for the studies of Fossey and Goodall. Biruté convinced him to secure funding for her to study orangutans in Borneo. The National Geographic Society, which funded the project, helped establish a research facility in Borneo. In 1986, Biruté cofounded the Orangutan Foundation International to provide worldwide support to orangutans. She has spent more than forty years in Borneo, contributing to significant scientific gains about the behavior of orangutans and advocating to preserve their natural habitat.

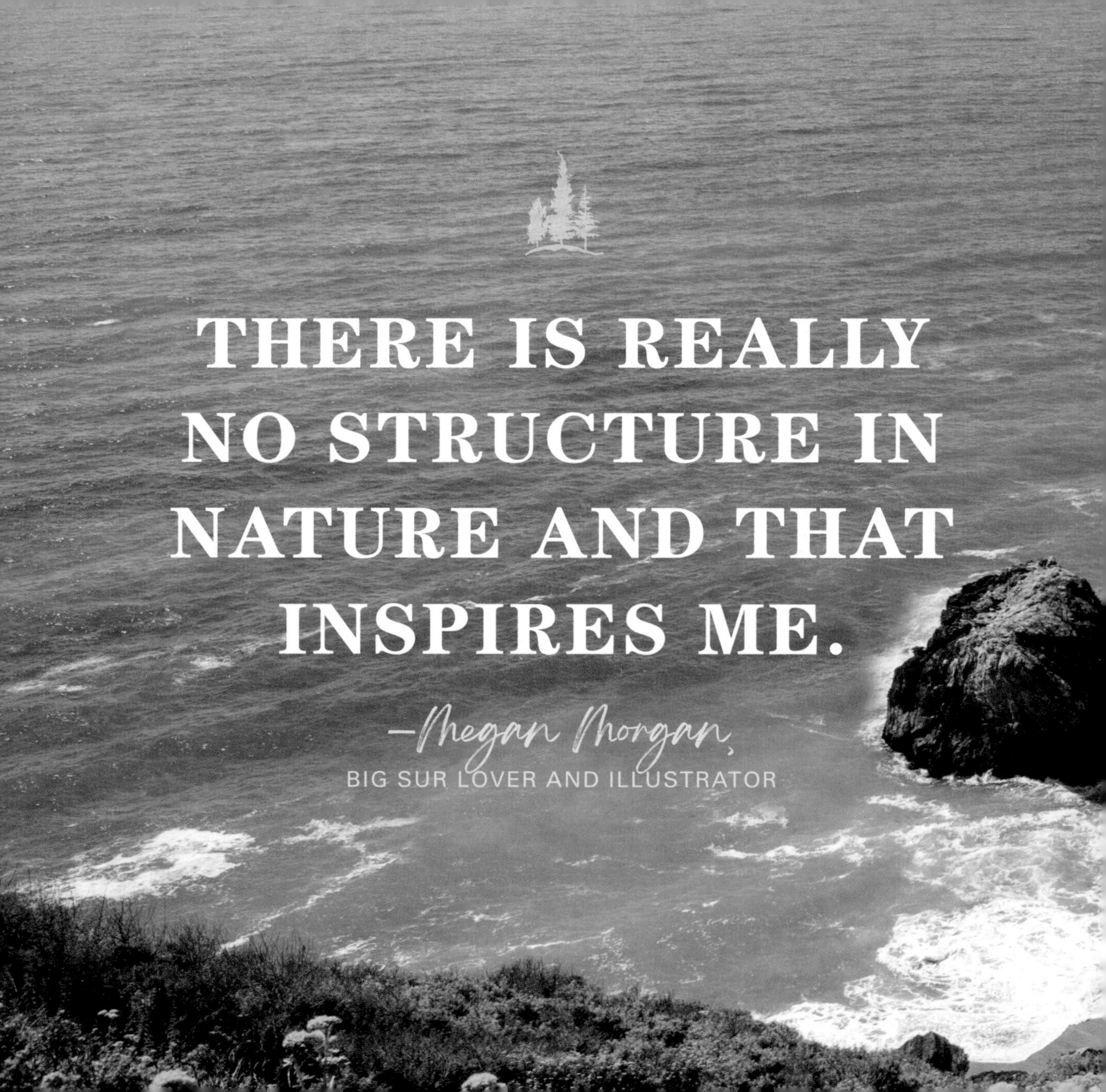
THERE IS REALLY NO STRUCTURE IN NATURE AND THAT INSPIRES ME.
—Megan Morgan,
BIG SUR LOVER AND ILLUSTRATOR

MEGAN MORGAN GREW UP IN A SMALL LAKE TOWN. When her mind would begin to jump around, she would take her journal down to the lake to sketch. It soothed her.

Time passed. She fell in love with a boy named Chris. She met his family in California. They drove on Highway 1, a winding road perched between craggy cliffsides and the foamy sea. She was enchanted and inspired by both the road and the man by her side.

Soon, they had two beautiful sons and her days were overflowing with love. They were also bound by structure: breakfasts and nap times, playdates and preschool, baths and bedtimes. Love flowed freely, but structure demanded she sacrifice inspiration.

Megan loved who she had become, but she missed who she had been.

She packed up the family and headed up Highway 1. They arrived at Big Sur, a place full of natural wonder. There was no structure; there didn't need to be. Nature's only rule was freedom and it's one that she and her family instinctively understood.

Once home, she felt her creativity return. She began to draw and found herself sketching the natural world in vibrant colors. She shares her happy art online, taking her own joy and multiplying it for others.

She learned that her happy place is the balancing point between motherhood and Mother Earth. Whenever she feels it slipping away, she packs up her family and jumps on the magical highway that takes them into the wilderness.

Say
yes to
adventure

15

FORGET NOT THAT THE EARTH DELIGHTS TO FEEL YOUR BARE FEET AND THE WINDS LONG TO PLAY WITH YOUR HAIR.

—Khalil Gibran

YOU WERE NOT MADE FOR A PREDICTABLE, THRILL-LESS LIFE.

You were created for adventure.

If you doubt this, think of the way your body and mind are meticulously constructed. Your body is full of bones and muscles and sinew and fat. It is made for moving and lifting and climbing and surviving. Your mind is full of neurons and synapses and electricity. It is made for learning and imagination and creativity and wonder.

You owe it to yourself, or at least to your body and your brain, to give in to adventure.

That's the beautiful thing about adventure. You don't have to seek it out. It is available around every corner just waiting for your enthusiastic response. When you hear adventure's call, just say, "Yes."

Once you are ready, put on a pair of sturdy shoes and weather-appropriate attire and head outside. Start there. Walk without a set destination. If you're walking in a neighborhood, try to get your feet off the sidewalk and onto the dirt. Let your feet and the muscles in your legs acclimate to uneven ground. Wake up your body by climbing up stairs, jumping off benches, skipping up a hill, and hanging from trees. Your body was created to do these very things. If you need a reminder, look at all of the ways that children use their body on a playground. They leap, swing, hop, crawl, shimmy, sprint, and crouch. That's because the body craves this kind of movement. Allow yourself to move the way you did as a child.

Let your mind experience the things around you as new and exciting. Simply taking the time to look around at your surroundings can be an adventure. If you always walk the same path, take a new turn or walk it backward. These small changes cause your mind to pay attention and engage with your surroundings. When you are stuck in a routine, your mind will disengage and go into autopilot. Any time you experience this autopilot mode, you can be sure that you are not on an adventure. An adventure forces your mind to look at things as new and exciting challenges and possibilities. It expands the way that you think.

As you spend more time outdoors, push yourself to go on new adventures that are within your reasonable skill set. If you like to walk, try going on a short hike on a well-marked trail. If you love to hike, try a new path that involves climbing over small boulders or ends with a vista you haven't experienced before. If you like to bike, take a new trail. If you like to meditate, find a new location with different smells, sights, and sounds.

Nature is full of infinite adventures. All you have to do is show up.

Environmental Action in the Early 2000s[15]

2000
30th anniversary of the original Earth Day

2001
A report on global warming prepared by the National Science Foundation is released

2002
In Johannesburg, South Africa, the World Summit on Sustainable Development happens

2004
Massive tsunamis are unleashed, killing 230,000, after a large earthquake under the Indian Ocean

2006
Al Gore releases *An Inconvenient Truth*

2008
World Glacier Monitoring Service reports that 30 glaciers they have been tracking are melting at an accelerated rate

Berta Isabel Cáceres Flores (1971–2016)

HONDURAN ENVIRONMENTAL ACTIVIST AND INDIGENOUS LEADER

Berta Flores's mother showed her what it meant to be an activist in Honduras. Her mother, Austra, was a humanitarian and a midwife who took in refugees from El Salvador. Austra was also a mayor for their hometown and a representative in congress. When Berta was nineteen, she cofounded the National Council of Popular and Indigenous Organizations of Honduras to protect the rights of her people from illegal logging. When the Gualcarque River, a sacred place to Berta's people, was going to be dammed, she organized a human blockade to stop construction. The blockade lasted for a year, and they continued to protest afterward. She was threatened with criminal charges and received kidnapping and murder threats. One of her protest leaders was killed and this resulted in the dam project being canceled and the Gualcarque River remained protected. Tragically, Berta was murdered in her home, but her memory still remains alive.

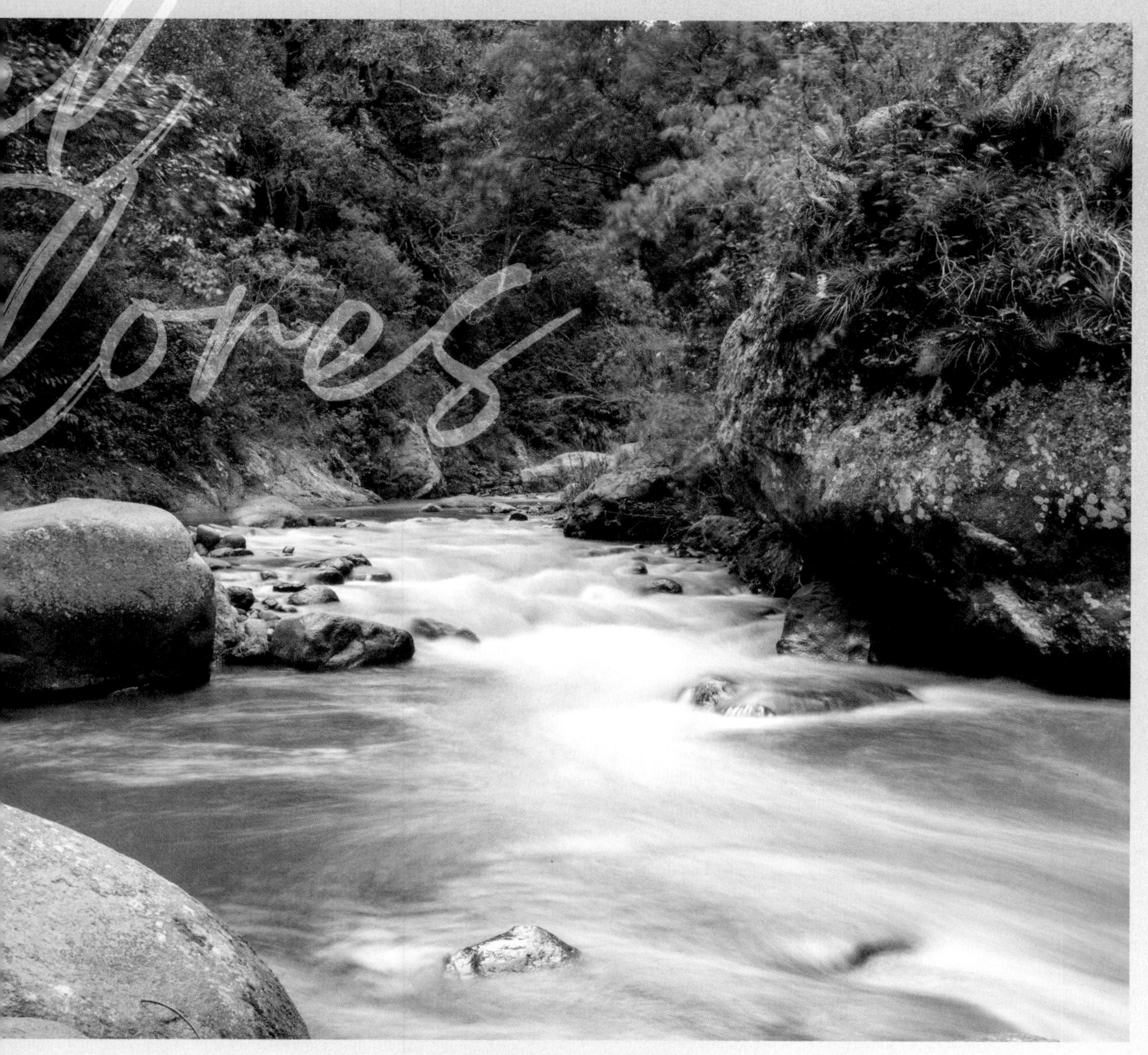

I [TRAVEL] ALONE SO I CAN HAVE A SPIRITUAL ENCOUNTER WITH NATURE AND NOT JUST A WALK.

—Amanda Rothman,
SOLO EXPLORER AND WORDSMITH

AMANDA ROTHMAN DECIDED TO HIKE THE FOOTHILLS OF THE ALPS. She booked a vacation rental in a charming mountain town so she could walk from her front door to the trail.

When Amanda arrived, she found the trail was far away and decided to take the bus. The Italian woman Amanda was renting the place from laughed knowingly, "Don't take the bus. It will never come. You're better off hitchhiking."

Amanda woke early the next day and waited by the side of the road. Sure enough, she was picked up.

Once at the trail, Amanda realized how jet-lagged she was. Against her better judgment, she started up the trail.

It was narrow and the trees were dense. Her exhaustion caused her to slip and fall; she saved herself by grabbing a tree. She made it to a clearing and saw a ramshackle stone shed. As she rounded the corner, she found herself face to face with a long-horned bull. They both froze. She inched by the bull, relieved until she realized she had lost the trail.

She tried to force her way through some shrubbery and became more disoriented. Defeated, she started to head down the mountain, but then somehow her feet found the trail.

She followed a series of switchbacks and made it to the summit. The view was exquisite. She had never felt so close to God. She started to cry when she realized that she had never been lost on this adventure; it was leading her exactly where she needed to be all along.

Make waves

16

WHATEVER YOU ARE BY NATURE, KEEP TO IT; NEVER DESERT YOUR LINE OF TALENT. BE WHAT NATURE INTENDED YOU FOR AND YOU WILL SUCCEED.

—Sydney Smith

YOUR GUT INSTINCT IS ONE OF YOUR *most powerful gifts.*

It might present itself as a literal feeling you get in your stomach or it might show up as a little voice inside of you that wants your attention.

Your gut instinct can be triggered when something good or bad is happening. It is like an internal alert system. Your gut instinct can alert you to a potential opportunity. You might suddenly feel excited, hopeful, or bold when this occurs. Your gut instinct can also alert you to a potential danger or to something that feels wrong. You might suddenly feel on edge, angry, or defensive.

There is only one thing you need to know about your gut instinct: listen to it. Your gut instinct exists to keep you in alignment with who you are and what your purpose is.

When your gut instinct kicks in, it's time to respond and take appropriate action. The action you take should be commensurate with the intensity of the gut instinct you experience. As nature is the best teacher, let's look to her to determine the appropriate strength of your response when your gut instinct tells you that it's time to make some waves.

If something feels slightly right or moderately "off," think of responding like waves gently lapping on the shore. The waves are present and make an impact, but they do it subtly. The sand that the wave leaves on the beach and the sand the wave takes away is done so gradually that it's almost unnoticeable. In a situation where your gut instinct is telling you that things are only slightly off, respond with grace and subtlety. Responding in this manner generates change slowly and over time.

If something feels obviously right or clearly wrong to you, think of responding like a wave that has the perfect barrel. A wave like this gives a skilled rider a satisfying ride that leaves them fulfilled and allows them to demonstrate their expertise. A wave like this is also powerful enough to toss someone who has not developed the necessary skills and reveals their weaknesses. If you respond with a respectable amount of power, you will get closer to your goal and remove any obstacles in your way. Responding in this manner allows you to make necessary changes efficiently.

If something feels enthusiastically right or egregiously wrong to you, think of responding like a tsunami. The ocean reserves this level of power for rare events. If there is something that shakes your core, through resonance or rejection, you are being called to respond in a powerful way. Responding in this manner creates massive change in your own life and can also impact the lives of others.

What kind of wave are you going to be today?

Marine Conservation Organizations[16]

1967

American Cetacean Society is founded to protect the habitats needed to sustain marine wildlife

1972

Ocean Conservancy is founded to clean the oceans and beaches

1977

Sea Shepherd is founded to stop poachers from depleting marine wildlife

2001

Oceana is founded to work on getting laws in place to protect the ocean

2005

Oceanic Preservation Society is founded to increase public awareness of the ocean's needs

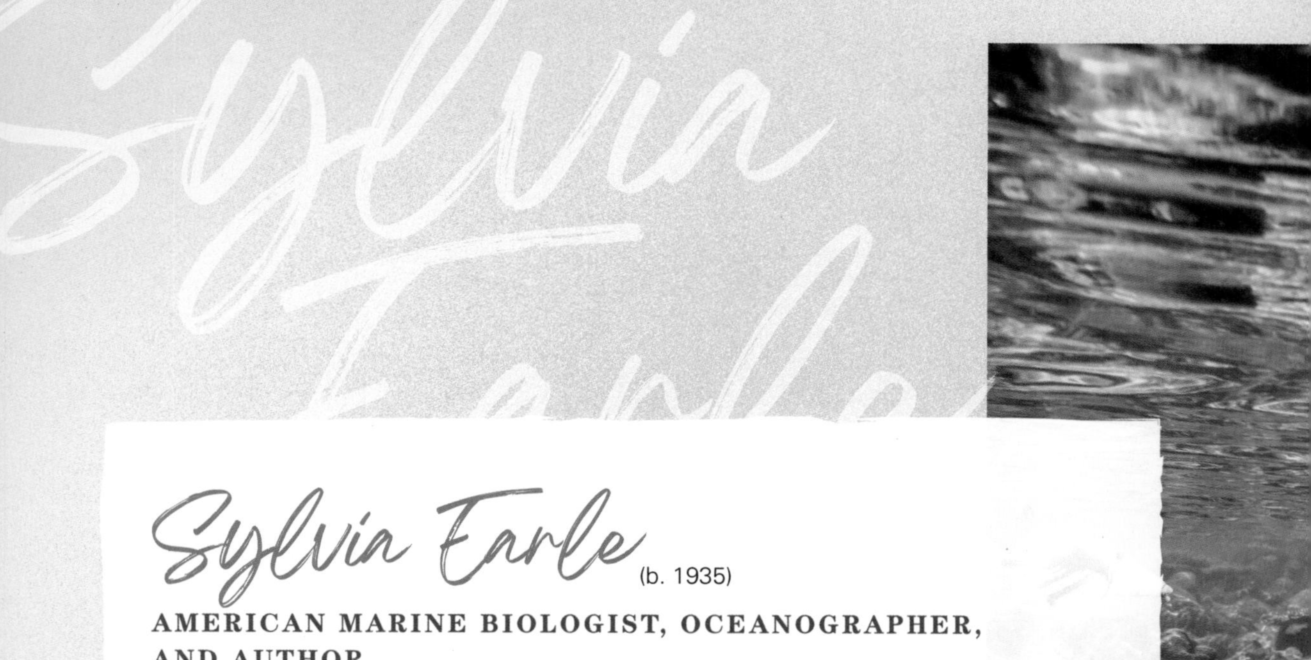

Sylvia Earle (b. 1935)

AMERICAN MARINE BIOLOGIST, OCEANOGRAPHER, AND AUTHOR

Sylvia Earle's parents encouraged her love of nature. They moved to the Florida coast when she was young. Once grown, she received a bachelor of science degree from Florida State University and a master of science and doctorate of phycology from Duke University. She went on to become a research associate at the University of California, Berkeley, and a research fellow at Harvard University. In 1979, she set the women's depth record for an open-ocean JIM suit dive 1,250 feet below the surface to the ocean floor. In 1982, she cofounded Deep Ocean Engineering to create and pilot robotic subsea systems. In 1985, they designed the Deep Rover research submarine. In 1990, Sylvia was the first woman ever appointed as the chief scientist at the National Oceanic and Atmospheric Administration. A National Geographic Explorer-in-Residence since 1998, she has earned the nickname "Her Deepness." In 2009, she founded Mission Blue and received a million-dollar prize for her ocean advocacy. In 2018, she received the Lifetime Achievement Award from the Seattle Aquarium.

THE FEELING OF STOKE IS SO REAL. IT'S LIKE THAT BUTTERFLY FEELING WHEN YOU GET SO EXCITED THAT YOU ACCOMPLISHED SOMETHING SO INCREDIBLE—YOU JUST ACHIEVED THIS MAJOR FEAT.

—*Melissa D'Anna,*
SURFER AND SURF-SHOP OWNER

MELISSA D'ANNA GREW UP ON THE JERSEY SHORE. When she was eleven, she started to surf. She didn't like being the only girl in surf camp, but her love of the waves kept her going.

After college, she moved to New York City to pursue her dream of being an actress. She booked a show in The-Middle-of-Nowhere, Kentucky, and was surprised to find that she preferred it to the concrete of the city. She now knew what she needed: nature and waves. She moved to Hawaii and blissfully spent her free time surfing.

After a magical year, she moved back to Jersey. The job market was fierce, and her closest friends had moved away. The once joy-filled Melissa was jobless, lonely, and depressed.

Melissa started to see a therapist. The therapist asked Melissa what made her happy.

Melissa remembered being the only little girl at the childhood surf camps she attended. She thought it would be wonderful to open a female-owned surf shop, but she had never run a business. Her therapist let her know that no one knows what they are doing—they just do it.

So, she did. She opened Lucky Dog Surf Co. and started Lucky Dog Surf School. Melissa no longer feels depressed because having a dream gave her purpose. She now sees as many, if not more, girls enrolled in her surf camps as boys. Melissa spends her days enjoying the waves: the ones she rides and the ones she has made in the industry.

Find
the calm
within

17

ADOPT THE PACE OF NATURE; HER SECRET IS PATIENCE.

—Ralph Waldo Emerson

CALM IS A *commodity.*

The prevalence of practices, supplements, workshops, practitioners, and products that claim to enhance your sense of inner peace are proof that there is a market demand for calmness. This means that there are a lot of people out there right now actively searching for inner peace.

You don't have to look far. You have the ability to turn to the greatest teacher of calm at any time. In fact, this teacher is thought of by some as the ultimate source of peace. This teacher is right outside your window. This teacher is nature.

Nature has a way of accepting, adapting, and acclimating to the many things that come her way. She has a deep knowing that she has the ability to heal from tragedy and to transmute devastation into new life. The trust that nature has in herself equates to an environment of calmness.

To embody this sense of calm, you can think about the following examples of calmness in nature. Try to incorporate some of their qualities into your own.

Think of a deep and tranquil lake. Imagine its fresh, blue, clear, and beautiful water. Though the top of the lake may be disrupted by the wind or frozen over by the cold, the depths of the water remain undisturbed. When external influences are impacting you, visualize your internal stability much like the deep waters of a lake: quiet, balanced, and still.

Think of fertile soil. Imagine its deep, rich, dark, and varied composition. This soil is formed over years of erosion and decomposition. Through time, this soil was perfectly made. By trusting time, this soil eventually has everything it needs to promote growth. When you are feeling like you do not have the tools you need and it makes you anxious, know that you are being perfected over time like the soil. You have what you need, when you need it, to grow.

Think of the animals. Imagine the way they wake and sleep with the sun and use their instincts to find food when needed. Animals trust that they will be provided for and trust themselves to know how to find what they need. When you feel lost or confused, remind yourself of the animals. As an animal yourself, you can trust that you have the skills you need and that the world is an abundant place.

Whenever the external world starts to feel overwhelming and you are seeking the calm within, just ask yourself: What would nature do?

Time Line of Early Environmental Education[17]

1836

"Nature," an essay by Ralph Waldo Emerson, explains the connection between humans and nature

1854

Walden, a book by Henry David Thoreau, is about going into nature to find true meaning

1891

Nature Study for the Common Schools, a book by Wilbur Jackman, shapes nature study

1903

Conservationist John Muir's writing helps educate others

1905

Handbook of Nature Study is written by Anna Botsford Comstock

Julia Butterfly Hill (b. 1974)

AMERICAN ACTIVIST AND AUTHOR

Julia Hill almost died in a car crash in 1996. This caused her to seek deeper meaning in her life. She found it in the redwoods. In December 1997, Julia took up residence in a thousand-year-old California redwood tree. The tree, known as Luna, was being threatened by the logging industry. Julia wanted to bring awareness to the atrocity of cutting down "ecologically significant forests." With the help of an organization called Earth First!, Julia was able to receive supplies and provisions that allowed her to live in Luna. She was determined. The logging corporation tried to get her to leave the tree by using floodlights and loudspeakers. She had to overcome the weather and sickness. She did not falter. Julia set the world record for the longest time tree-sitting by living in Luna for 738 days. At the end of her stay, Luna was saved, as were her immediate surroundings. She also earned a $50,000 donation for forestry research granted to Humboldt State University.

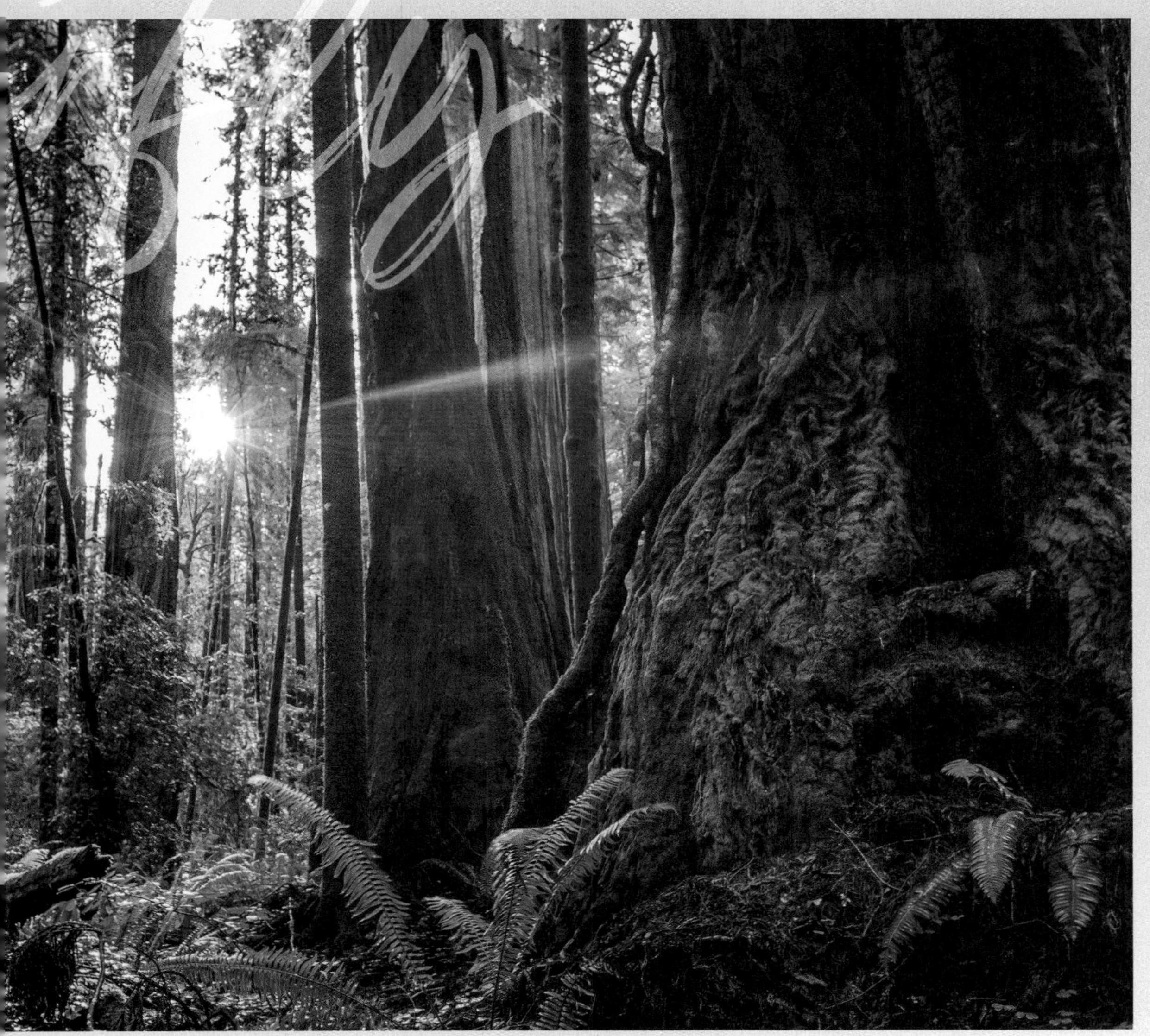

BEING OUTSIDE AND WALKING IN NATURE, BREATHING IN THE FRESH AIR, FEELING THE WIND ON MY FACE, AND HEARING THE BIRDS CHIRP PUTS ME AT PEACE SO MUCH THAT IT'S HARD TO PUT INTO WORDS.

—*Sara Spangler,*

MARINE BIOLOGIST AND YOGA AFICIONADO

THE BEACH HAS BEEN A PART OF SARA SPANGLER'S LIFE FROM THE BEGINNING. Growing up on Long Island meant that she was always surrounded by water. She loved to spend her free time outside by the ocean.

In college, she double majored in marine biology and environmental science. She then moved to Florida to work on coral restoration. She was very happy with her job because it allowed her to be near the beach full time. In Sara's free time, she began to do yoga. She loved the variety of wellness benefits she received. When the pandemic began, with its accompanying stressors, Sara made the conscious decision to be more consistent with her time on the yoga mat.

She noticed her mental state improving. After each yoga session, she found increased clarity and more energy. It reminded her of the way she felt after a day at the beach.

She realized that yoga and nature provided similar benefits, and both vastly improved her mental state. She found that yoga and nature paired easily because they are both about remaining present and mindful. She decided to combine the two. She began waking up and heading outside to start her day with yoga straight away.

After experiencing the benefits of yoga in nature, Sara couldn't keep the beach-in-a-bottle feeling to herself. She is currently building a yoga community online that combines nature with the practice of yoga to help people find the calm that she has found. It turns out she carried the beach inside of her all along.

Connect with the Trees

18

THE TREE WHICH MOVES SOME TO TEARS OF JOY IS IN THE EYES OF OTHERS ONLY A GREEN THING THAT STANDS IN THE WAY. SOME SEE NATURE ALL RIDICULE AND DEFORMITY...AND SOME SCARCE SEE NATURE AT ALL. BUT TO THE EYES OF THE MAN OF IMAGINATION, NATURE IS IMAGINATION ITSELF.

—William Blake

THERE IS SO MUCH TO LEARN *from a tree.*

It is nature's perfect example of determination, resilience, patience, and power.

When a tree first begins to grow, it is weak and vulnerable. It relies on nature to provide it with the light, water, and food it needs to grow. Sometimes it is blessed with a canopy of other trees to assist with its growth. Sometimes a tree grows alone and must withstand the elements without protection. The tree continues to make every effort to stretch its branches skyward, regardless of the conditions, because it was *born to grow*. This is much like the upbringing of a human. Some people are blessed with a large, protective, and nurturing family to help shield them from their growing pains. Other people are born alone and unprotected from the elements. Regardless of the vastly different circumstances, the birthright of both is to grow.

As the tree perseveres, it becomes taller. As the tree grows upward, it also grows downward. The strength and depth of the tree's underground root system determines how tall and wide the tree can grow. Your root system is represented by all of the unseen influences in your life that provide foundation and support. This might be your family or friends who have become family. Your root system is also composed of what you have learned in your life, your education, and your values. If you are seeking to grow, take the time to nurture the elements of your root system.

As the tree ages, it becomes wiser and stronger. Think of an ancient tree with a strong, layered, weathered, and durable trunk. Each ring within the tree represents perseverance. These rings lead to greater stability. The outside of the tree, bearing the scars of survival, provides it with protection. Each experience the tree has had has made it exactly what it is today. Remember that all of your experiences, even those that may cause you to feel shame or sadness or confusion, resulted in layers of learning inside of you; this is the wisdom you have earned. It has also helped you build a layer of protection between yourself and unwanted external influences; you have also earned this emotional armor with all of its beautiful scars.

As the tree exists, it experiences a variety of seasons. It may bloom in spring, be full of vibrant green leaves in summer, burst into fiery shades in autumn, and appear barren in winter. The tree is no more or less of itself in its varying seasonal iterations; it exists exactly as it was intended to. As you go through the different seasons of your life, some of abundance and joy and others of desolation and pain, remember that you are no more or less of yourself in each of these seasons. You have everything you need to survive and it is only a matter of time before you bloom yet again.

Your growth, wisdom, strength, and the seasons in your life are all things that you can more clearly comprehend when you connect with the trees.

Time Line of Modern Environmental Education[18]

2002

The Johannesburg Summit brings together thousands of people to educate the world on natural resources

2004

Wangari Maathai, the Kenyan environmentalist responsible for the Greenbelt Movement, wins the Nobel Peace Prize

2008

The U.S. House of Representatives passes the No Child Left Inside Act

2011

The U.S. Department of Education begins to issue Green Ribbon School Awards

2016

The Global Environmental Education Partnership, which focuses on environmental literacy, is formed

Wangari Maathai (1940–2011)

POLITICAL ACTIVIST, ENVIRONMENTALIST, AND AUTHOR

Wangari Maathai was from a rural community in Kenya. In 1961, she attended college in the United States, receiving a degree in biological sciences from a school in Kansas and later a master of science from the University of Pittsburgh. She continued to pursue education in Germany and Nairobi, ultimately earning her PhD, which made her the first woman in the central and eastern areas of Africa to ever receive a doctorate degree. She became the Department Chair of Veterinary Anatomy at the University of Nairobi. While she was the acting chairwoman for the National Council of Women of Kenya, she founded the Green Belt Movement to help both the environment and those in poverty through community-based tree planting. In 2004, she received the Nobel Peace Prize. She has also written four books about the environment, the state of her continent, and her autobiography.

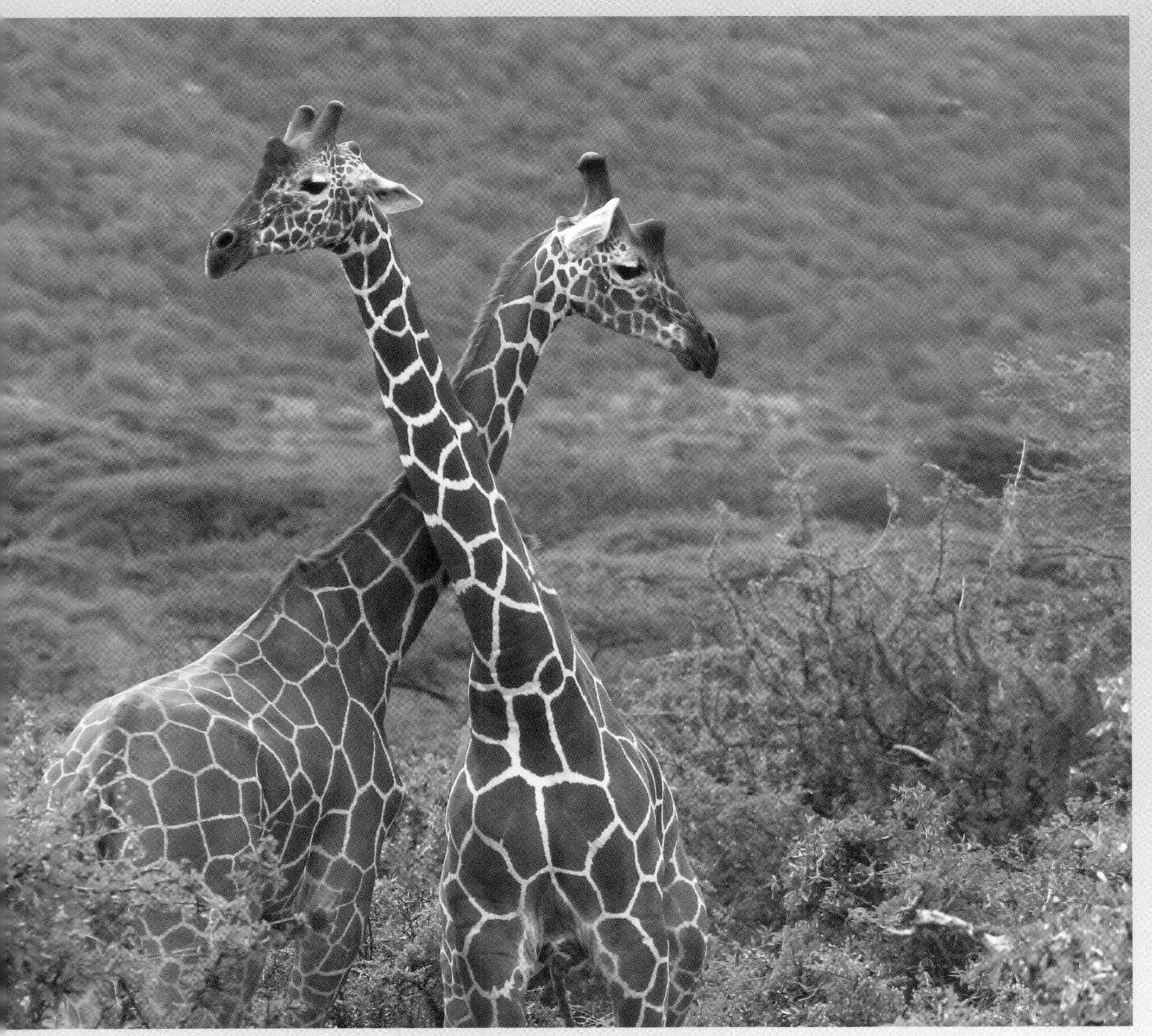

RUNNING IN THE FOREST WITH ALL THE BIRDS AROUND ME HELPS ME CLEAR MY MIND AND RECONNECT TO NATURE.

—Jessica Lamb,

TREE LOVER AND CROSS-COUNTRY RUNNER

WHEN SHE WAS TWELVE YEARS OLD, JESSICA LAMB STARTED CROSS-COUNTRY RUNNING. It wasn't easy, but she was hooked. Her father helped her train by taking her running in the forest near their home. At fifteen, she was running competitively.

Jessica found herself running the forest trail six days a week and biking it on the seventh. She felt the need to spend time with the trees of the forest every single day.

The trees that surrounded her felt like friends. The sound of the birds in the trees was her calming song. The earth beneath her feet was her favorite running path. It was all so beautiful—but the best part was the way it made her feel. At the midway point of her run, the feeling would appear. Some people refer to this blissful feeling as a "runner's high;" for Jessica, it was more akin to the feeling of nirvana achieved during meditation. She felt her mind clear and reconnect to the trees around her.

Nature gave her a sense of peace. Because of that, she wanted to give nature that sense of peace in return. She started doing conservation work to fix the ways that humans have harmed nature. Conservation work gave her purpose.

She wants generations to come to experience the magic that happens when you run deep into a forest with only the trees as your companions. She knows that others deserve the two life-altering gifts that the trees have given to her: peace and purpose.

Bloom like a flower

19

EVERY FLOWER IS A SOUL BLOSSOMING IN NATURE.

—Gérard de Nerval

THERE IS A MINDSET PRACTICE THAT CAN INCREASE YOUR *life satisfaction.*

If you continue to incorporate this practice, it will become a more frequent state of mind. This mindset leads to peace, contentment, and understanding. This is the mindset of forgiveness.

Forgiveness is the conscious decision to let go of resentment, anger, and vengeful thoughts toward another. Though this may sound simple, forgiving someone can be incredibly difficult to do. It is natural to think that someone who has wronged you does not deserve your forgiveness. If you fall into this line of thinking, lean into the understanding that forgiveness is an act of goodness on your part and it also frees you from carrying the weight of negative thoughts. Think of the times in your life that you have felt or expressed genuine forgiveness. If a flower bloomed each time you had a moment of intentional forgiveness, what would the garden of your life look like?

Perhaps you are someone who constantly focuses on who has wronged you, things that didn't go your way, and the ways in which you want to exact revenge. This might lead you to the belief that people are bad, that the cards are stacked against you. Or you may spend time planning how to harm someone whom you believe has harmed you. You might end up angry and bitter. The garden of your life would likely appear barren, empty, or dead.

Perhaps you are someone who is forgiving at times and holds a grudge at other times. You have days when you believe in the good of humanity and others when you think people are rotten. The garden of your life likely has some very beautiful flowers, but you might not notice them through all of the weeds.

Perhaps you are someone who actively practices forgiveness. When someone wrongs you, you tap into your compassion, empathy, and grace to reach a place of understanding or to let it go. You have generated the wisdom to truly understand what the Buddha meant when he said, "Holding on to anger is like grasping a hot coal with the intent of throwing it at someone else; you are the one who gets burned." The garden of your life is likely well-tended, bursting with color, and full of butterflies, hummingbirds, and bees.

To prioritize forgiveness, make a habit of practicing it. Start by forgiving yourself for anything you are holding on to. Allow yourself to acknowledge that you are a human being who makes mistakes and that you are deserving of mercy. Once you learn how to forgive yourself, you can generate the empathy needed to forgive others.

Once you dedicate yourself to practicing forgiveness, the garden of your life will come into full bloom.

Home Gardening in the U.S. from the 1950s Onward[19]

1950s to 1960s

The creation of home-use pesticides influences gardening techniques

1970s

The idea of edible landscaping, or gardens that are beautiful and edible, and urban community gardens take center stage

1980s

People become aware of using drought-tolerant and native vegetation

1990s

Urban gardening grows in popularity as more and more people move to the cities

2000s

An increasing awareness of the benefits of local, fresh food leads to an increase in edible gardens

Anna Botsford Comstock (1854–1930)

AMERICAN AUTHOR, ILLUSTRATOR, AND EDUCATOR

While at Cornell University, Anna Botsford met John Henry Comstock, an entomologist; he was someone who studied insects. She left school and married him. Through John, she became interested in insect illustration. She assisted him without pay until he became the chief entomologist for the U.S. Department of Agriculture. She received a paid position to draw citrus scale insects. She then re-enrolled in Cornell and earned a degree in natural history. She coauthored and illustrated many books on insects with her husband. She also authored and illustrated many books on insects, nature, and animals on her own. She was appointed to the New York State Committee for the Promotion of Agriculture and created the nature study framework for the schools throughout New York State. By 1897, she was the first female professor at Cornell.

I LOVE WHEN A GARDEN STARTS TO BLOOM. THIS MEANS THAT THE GARDEN IS EXPERIENCING AN EMOTION; IT FEELS HAPPY.

—Karla Ovalle,
LOVER OF BEAUTY AND EMPATH

KARLA OVALLE COMES FROM A FAMILY OF METAPHORICAL FLOWERS. Some family members are delicate and soft. Others are showy and bright. Some are "seedy." She knows her family thinks of her as a flower, too. That's why they gave her the name "Little Rose."

The name fit her; Karla had always been beautiful, but she could not see it.

There were reasons for this. The older flowers whom she looked to for love spat back with envy-laden insults. Other flowers were too busy protecting themselves to notice she was struggling to grow.

Her petals began to wilt. She watched the flowers fight over decaying food so that they could bloom. She thought, "Flowers are fed ugly things so they can be beautiful."

Karla thought about all of the ugly things she had been fed; maybe they would make her beautiful. This thought allowed her to feel grateful for the ugly food her family of flowers had fed her. This gratitude led to empathy. This empathy led to understanding. This understanding became forgiveness.

In a garden full of selfish flowers, Karla saw the beauty in their wilted petals. She focused so much on their beauty that she didn't notice them staring in shock at her own. Her petals were open to the sun. Her stem was strong and her thorns were few.

They didn't know how she had done it. None of them had been watered in ages. She realized that they hadn't gone deep enough. The well of forgiveness had been there all along.

Thank Mother Earth

20

NATURE'S BEAUTY IS A GIFT THAT CULTIVATES APPRECIATION AND GRATITUDE.

—Louie Schwartzberg

THE SAYING *"misery loves company"* EXISTS BECAUSE MISERY CAN ONLY BE FUELED BY MORE MISERY.

On the flip side, *the greatest antidote to misery is gratitude.*

This is true because you cannot experience misery at the same time as gratitude. If you shift your mind to a state of gratitude, you will eradicate the misery you are experiencing at that moment.

Think about how you feel when you are having a horrible week. The kind of week where you don't want to get out of bed or let light into your room. The kind of week where you don't want to talk to anyone or do anything. The kind of week where everything seems gray, pointless, and miserable.

If you give in to your instincts—not getting out of bed, not letting any light in, not talking to anyone, and not doing anything—you can guarantee that your life will, in fact, feel gray, pointless, and miserable.

If you fight your instincts—getting out of bed, letting natural light in, calling someone who cares, and getting out to do something—you will likely discover that your life is not as gray, pointless, and miserable as you had previously assumed.

The problem is that Misery tends to travel with Lack of Motivation, so it might feel downright impossible to get out of bed. Instead, accept that you aren't getting out of bed. Now, grab something to write with; your phone works just fine. Label the top of the page "Things I Am Grateful For." Then start to write a numbered list.

Do not expect the gears of gratitude to be well-oiled initially; you might struggle to have something listed next to "1." Just start small. Write something like "food" or "the gift of sight" or "having a mattress to rest on." Conscious gratitude reminds you of the things you have taken for granted that someone else wants.

Continue writing until you cannot think of anything else. The list usually ends up being longer than you thought. That's the thing with the gears of gratitude: they lock up when they aren't used often but, once moving, they generate incredible momentum.

Odds are high that many of the things on your list have to do with nature. Maybe you thought of sunshine, water, the beach, the forest, mountains, sunsets, animals, trees, flowers, or the moon. Maybe you didn't and now you have even more things to add to your gratitude list.

Now, get out of bed. You have too many colorful things to be grateful for to waste another moment in the gray. And, if you aren't going to make it outside today, at least open your window. Take a moment to look outside and say, "Thank you." If all you've done today is thank Mother Earth for all she has done for you, you've done enough.

Farming of Fish[20]

1733
Aquaculture, or our version of modern fish farming, appears in Germany

1899
Western countries establish fish hatcheries

1924
Tilapia is raised en masse in Kenyan ponds

1950
Plastic is introduced and becomes a go-to material for fish farming

1959
The Vik brothers create cages for ocean-based fish farming

1970
The world's first successful salmon farm launches

2018
Chile earns a patent for a self-propelled fish farm

Rachel Carson

Rachel Carson (1907–1964)

SCIENTIST AND AUTHOR

Rachel Carson was raised in a rural town in Pennsylvania. Through her studies, she eventually earned a master's degree in zoology from Johns Hopkins University. She was hired by the U.S. Bureau of Fisheries and eventually became editor-in-chief for the U.S. Fish and Wildlife Service. She wrote numerous books about the ocean; she gave readers an inside look at life on, under, and around the ocean. This allowed many people to have an understanding of the ecology of the ocean for the very first time. She taught people about island formation, the effect of erosion on the ocean, the different microorganisms in the ocean, and how temperature changes impact the ocean climate. Her most famous work, *Silent Spring*, was a book that questioned the agricultural pesticide use implemented by the government. Her final act before her death was testifying before Congress demanding new policies to protect people against pesticide use.

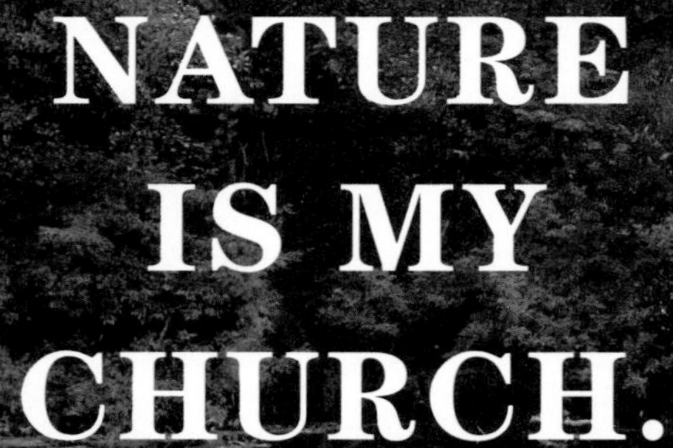

NATURE IS MY CHURCH.

—Kalee McCormick,

DAUGHTER OF MOTHER EARTH AND GRATITUDE GIVER

KALEE MCCORMICK'S CHILDHOOD WAS MARKED BY INSTABILITY. To navigate this, she would spend her days at the lake comforted by the sunshine. Nature was her safe place.

When Kalee reached adulthood, she experienced all-consuming hopelessness. She did not see the purpose of living. She was diagnosed with bipolar disorder. Kalee did not know how to navigate her thoughts and heal. She knew she needed her safe place.

She reorganized her life to make nature a priority. The time she spent outdoors gave her the healing she had hoped for. Nature had become more than her safe place; it was her sanctuary.

While in nature, Kalee spent time in stillness. She became aware that the plants, animals, and herself were all connected. She found this deep knowing to be incredibly healing. She had a spiritual transformation once she understood that we "are all one with nature." Nature became more than her sanctuary; she now refers to it as her church.

Her spiritual transformation led her to a space of deep gratitude. Each day, she thanks the Earth for her life; she knows that nature saved her.

Her goal is for others to learn what she has learned. She dreams of starting an organization with a focus on the interconnectedness of humanity and nature. Kalee wants others to have a life that is full of purpose and meaning. She knows that the path to this kind of a life involves protecting and giving thanks for the ultimate healer: Mother Earth.

Make a Positive Environmental Impact

It's important that we take care of Mother Earth. Here are some things you can do to protect the environment and provide a better future for generations to come.

- Become a Happy Earth Ambassador and take part in their monthly challenges.
- Educate yourself on environmental issues. Read books, search online, attend lectures, or watch documentaries.
- Be mindful of the environmental resources you are consuming and try to minimize your impact.
- Make one sustainable change at a time.
- Pick up trash wherever you see it.
- Properly sort your trash bins and reuse anything you can.
- Eliminate as much single-use plastic (think straws, zip-top bags, or food wrapped or packaged in plastic) from your life as possible.
- Have a compassionate conversation to educate others about the environment. Do it in a way that makes it understandable for them. Do not be aggressive or combative.
- Participate in an Earth Day volunteer event.
- Organize a beach or park cleanup.
- Practice proper "leave no trace" etiquette when spending time outdoors. Leave the place just as, or better than, you found it. Do not litter and do not take things from nature.
- Join or start organizations focused on the environment and sustainability at your school or university, or in your community.
- Start an eco-friendly social media page.
- Make the switch to reusable grocery and produce bags.

- Use the internet and social media to find local environmental events you can take part in.
- Save up and spend a little more on organic food. This is an investment in yourself, the environment, and sustainable farming practices.
- Restrict or remove animals and animal products from your diet. The University of Oxford found that becoming vegan can reduce your carbon footprint by 73 percent.
- If eating meat or poultry, make sure that it is "Animal Welfare Approved." This ensures that the animals are treated humanely and sustainably. It requires that animals are raised on a pasture or a range and the approval is only granted to independent farmers. You can find "Animal Welfare Approved" butchers to source your meat.
- Start a backyard garden. Use your own compost.
- Reduce your pollution. When thinking about the pollution you create, also consider noise and light pollution.
- Avoid fast fashion. Buy clothing items that are part of the slow fashion movement or available resale or exchange clothing with family or friends. Donate clothes you don't need anymore.
- Spend time outdoors. Connecting with nature is good for you and for the environment.

List of Featured Contributors

Each chapter features a story about a real woman's personal experience with nature. The names and social media handles and/or websites (if applicable) of each woman included in the book are listed below.

CHAPTER 1: Samantha Yazzie
CHAPTER 2: Suzan Chiang • www.happymomblogger.com
CHAPTER 3: Stormy Light • @stormyella
CHAPTER 4: Kaitlyn Lamb • @kaitlyngrowz
CHAPTER 5: Muqu Javad • @muqu_ j
CHAPTER 6: Maggie Dewane • @mmdewane • www.maggiedewane.com
CHAPTER 7: Kirsten Foss
CHAPTER 8: Danielle Lovett • @dlovet01
CHAPTER 9: Haley Coffin
CHAPTER 10: Layna F. • @earthfriendlyjourney
CHAPTER 11: Kaitland Sweet
CHAPTER 12: Victoria Gennaro
CHAPTER 13: Yvesanniah Lacoude
CHAPTER 14: Megan Morgan • @meghalffull
CHAPTER 15: Amanda Rothman
CHAPTER 16: Melissa D'Anna • @luckydogsurf • www.luckydogsurf.com
CHAPTER 17: Sara Spangler • @palmtreeyogawithsara
CHAPTER 18: Jessica Lamb • @eco_runawayjess
CHAPTER 19: Karla Ovalle
CHAPTER 20: Kalee McCormick

References

"About Jane" (2019). Jane Goodall Institute. https://www.janegoodall.org/our-story/about-jane/#mentor.

"Anna Botsford Comstock" (2021). *Encyclopædia Britannica*. https://www.britannica.com/biography/Anna-Botsford-Comstock.

"Biruté Galdikas" (2021). Wikipedia. https://en.wikipedia.org/wiki/Birut%C3%A9_Galdikas.

Brandman (2021). "Biography: Winona LaDuke." National Women's History Museum. https://www.womenshistory.org/education-resources/biographies/winona-laduke.

1 "Controlled Burning" (2019). National Geographic Society. https://www.nationalgeographic.org/encyclopedia/controlled-burning.

3 David DiSalvo (2013). "Breathing and Your Brain: Five Reasons to Grab the Controls." *Forbes*. https://www.forbes.com/sites/daviddisalvo/2013/05/14/breathing-and-your-brain-five-reasons-to-grab-the-controls/?sh=640df5622d95.

"Dian Fossey" (2021). Wikipedia. https://en.wikipedia.org/wiki/Dian_Fossey.

"Douglas, Marjory Stoneman" (2021). National Women's Hall of Fame. https://www.womenofthehall.org/inductee/marjory-stoneman-douglas.

4 "Inspiration Definition & Meaning" (2021). *Merriam-Webster Dictionary*. https://www.merriam-webster.com/dictionary/inspiration#learn-more.

"Isatou Ceesay Wins 2020 Inspiration Award from the Gambia's Women's Chamber of Commerce" (2020). One Plastic Bag. http://oneplasticbag.com.

Kate Sessions" (2021). Wikipedia. https://en.wikipedia.org/wiki/Kate_Sessions.

Korrien Hopkins (2018). "The Legacy of Berta Càceres." UMKC Women's Center. https://info.umkc.edu/womenc/2018/03/19/the-legacy-of-berta-caceres.

"L. Hunter Lovins" (2019). Natural Capitalism Solutions. https://natcapsolutions.org/l-hunter-lovins.

Linda Lear (2015). "Rachel Carson's Biography." RachelCarson.org. https://www.rachelcarson.org/Bio.aspx.

"Margaret Murie" (2021). *Encyclopædia Britannica*. https://www.britannica.com/biography/Margaret-Murie.

Nessim Watson (2021). "Julia Butterfly Hill." *Encyclopædia Britannica*. https://www.britannica.com/biography/Julia-Butterfly-Hill.

Olivia Petter (2020). "Going Vegan Is 'Single Biggest Way' to Reduce Our Impact, Study Finds." The Independent. https://www.independent.co.uk/life-style/health-and-families/veganism-environmental-impact-planet-reduced-plant-based-diet-humans-study-a8378631.html.

"Rosalie Edge" (2021). Wikipedia. https://en.wikipedia.org/wiki/Rosalie_Edge.

"Saalumarada Thimmakka" (2021). Wikipedia. https://en.wikipedia.org/wiki/Saalumarada_Thimmakka.

"Sunita Narain" (2021). Centre for Science and Environment. https://www.cseindia.org/page/sunita-narain.

"Sylvia Earle" (2021). Wikipedia. https://en.wikipedia.org/wiki/Sylvia_Earle.

"The Circular Economy at COP26" (2021). Ellen MacArthur Foundation. https://ellenmacarthurfoundation.org.

"Vandana Shiva" (2021). Wikipedia. https://en.wikipedia.org/wiki/Vandana_Shiva.

"Wangari Maathai—Biography" (2021). The Green Belt Movement. https://www.greenbeltmovement.org/wangari-maathai/biography.

2 "Wildfire Causes and Evaluations (U.S. National Park Service)" (2021). National Parks Service, U.S. Department of the Interior. https://www.nps.gov/articles/wildfire-causes-and-evaluation.htm.

TIME LINES

1 "Turning 100: Major Milestones in the National Park Service" (2021). U.S. Department of the Interior. https://www.doi.gov/blog/turning-100-major-milestones-national-park-service.

2 "Bee Life Cycle—Different Stages of Honey Bee and Queen Bee" (2021). How to Get Rid of Bees Naturally without Harming Them. https://www.howtogettingridofbees.com/bee-life-cycle-different-stages-of-honey-bee-and-queen-bee.

3 "Mount Shasta" (2021). Wikipedia. https://en.wikipedia.org/wiki/Mount_Shasta.

4 "A New Century: 1900–1909" (2021). Environmental History. https://environmentalhistory.org/progressive/a-new-century-1900–1910.

5 "The 11 Biggest Volcanic Eruptions in History" (2016) Live Science. https://www.livescience.com/30507-volcanoes-biggest-history.html.

6 "History of the Soil Conservation" (2021). https://www.ag.ndsu.edu/ndssc/documents/HistoryoftheSoilConservation.pdf/view

7 "Timeline of Carbon Capture and Storage" (2021). Wikipedia. https://en.wikipedia.org/wiki/Timeline_of_carbon_capture_and_storage.

8 "Extinction over Time" (2021). Smithsonian National Museum of Natural History. https://naturalhistory.si.edu/education/teaching-resources/paleontology/extinction-over-time.

9 "List of Environmental Films" (2021). Wikipedia. https://en.wikipedia.org/wiki/List_of_environmental_films.

10 "9 of the Biggest Oil Spills in History." John Rafferty (2021). Encyclopædia Britannica. https://www.britannica.com/list/9-of-the-biggest-oil-spills-in-history.

11 "Prehistoric" (2017). Environmental History. https://environmentalhistory.org/ancient/prehistoric.